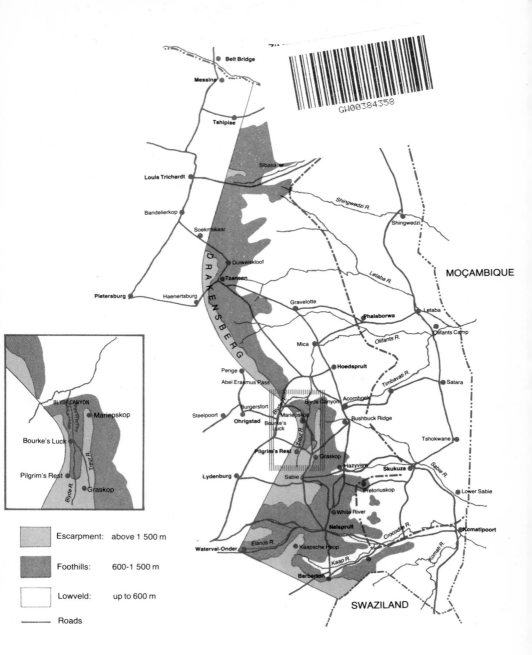

Belt Bridge

Messina

Tshipise

Sibasa

Louis Trichardt

Bandelierkop

Soekmekaar

Duiwelskloof

Tzaneen

Pietersburg

Haenertsburg

Shingwedzi R.

Shingwedzi

MOÇAMBIQUE

Gravelotte

Letaba R.

Phalaborwa

Letaba

Olifants Camp

Mica

Olifants R.

Hoedspruit

Penge

Abel Erasmus Pass

Timbavati R.

Satara

Steelpoort

Burgersfort

Blyde Canyon

Acornhoek

Ohrigstad

Mariepskop

Bourke's Luck

Bushbuck Ridge

Tshokwane

Pilgrim's Rest

Graskop

Hazyview

Skukuza

Sabie R.

Lydenburg

Sabie

Pretoriuskop

Lower Sabie

White River

Nelspruit

Crocodile R.

Komatipoort

Komati R.

Waterval-Onder

Elands R.

Kaapsche Hoop

Kaap R.

Barberton

SWAZILAND

D R A K E N S B E R G

Blyde Canyon inset

BLYDE CANYON

Mariepskop

Bourke's Luck

Treur R.

Pilgrim's Rest

Blyde R.

Graskop

	Escarpment:	above 1 500 m
	Foothills:	600–1 500 m
	Lowveld:	up to 600 m
	Roads	

TRANSVAAL LOWVELD
AND ESCARPMENT
including
THE KRUGER NATIONAL PARK

Transvaal Lowveld and Escarpment

including

the Kruger National Park

South African
Wild Flower Guide 4

JO ONDERSTALL

This guide is the fourth
in a series of Wild Flower Guides
published by the Botanical Society
of South Africa

The Botanical Society of South Africa was founded in 1913 to support the National Botanic Gardens and to promote the conservation and cultivation of our indigenous flora.

One of our projects is the publication of a series of wild flower guides.

Already published and in production are:

Namaqualand & Clanwilliam	1981
Outeniqua Tsitsikamma & eastern Little Karoo	1982
Cape Peninsula	1983
Transvaal Lowveld & Escarpment	1984
Hottentots Holland to Hermanus	1985

These and future guides will eventually cover most of the wild flower regions of South Africa.

For further information about the Botanical Society and its membership, please see the inside back cover.

List of Donors to Lowveld Guide

J. Rae	R100,00
SAPPI	R200,00
Beth Glass	R100,00
Mt Sheba Hotels and Nature Reserve	R100,00
Makhonjwa Cons. Foundation	R500,00
	R1 000,00

Published in 1984
Botanical Society of South Africa

© Text Jo Onderstall

Set, printed and bound by CTP Book Printers, Cape
Reproduction by Doble & Nagel (Pty) Ltd, Cape Town

ISBN 0 620 07749 2
BD2586

Opposite title page: A quiet mountain stream.

Message by the Honourable Minister S. A. S. Hayward MP and the Honourable Minister J. W. E. Wiley MP

To many South Africans the word 'Lowveld' conjures up an image of trackless bushveld populated by teeming wildlife: a vision of Eden, where animals have the right of way. It is an image that has been with us ever since 1898 when that wise, far-sighted President of the Zuid Afrikaansche Republiek, Paul Kruger, took the first steps towards the creation of the great national park that now bears his name.

With such an exceptional abundance of animal life capturing the limelight, it is perhaps only natural that the equally magnificent flora of the Lowveld and adjacent escarpment has tended to be of secondary interest to many naturalists. Part of the problem has been that there have been no good regional guides to the plant life of this area.

However, every year brings with it a greater, better-informed public, hungry for knowledge of our country's natural heritage. The big-game, birds, reptiles and trees of the lowveld have all been well documented in several excellent publications, but until now there has been no general layman's guide to the flora as a whole. This beautifully illustrated book fills a very real void in the popular literature. By supporting the Botanical Society of South Africa's excellent series of local field guides, my Department is hopeful that these reasonably priced publications will reach the widest possible audience.

Other issues in this series have already gone far towards informing South Africans of the wonderful natural plant life this land has been blessed with, as well as encouraging them to protect and conserve that flora and to be aware that plants are the ultimate primary producers upon which all life on earth depends.

S.A. Hayward

John Wiley

5

Contents

◀ The spectacular seed pod of the Kudu Lily *(Pachypodium saundersii).*

Overleaf: Typical of the Transvaal are the glowing red flowers of the Weeping Fuchsia *(Schotia brachypetala).*

Preface

This book — the fourth in the series of guidebooks on South African plants published by the Publications Committee of the Botanical Society — is the first to deal with a region outside the Cape Province. As these guidebooks are based on species diversity, it seems logical that it should be the Transvaal Lowveld and the adjacent escarpment to which the highest priority is given in the Transvaal.

There is no reliable information available on the number of plant species found in this area, but if it is kept in mind that more than 2 000 species have been found in the Kruger Park alone, it can be assumed that the geographic area as a whole could accommodate more than 3 000 species. The mere choice of species to be included in the publication to give readers a general idea of the flora, was a mammoth task. It was therefore vital to get an author with a sound knowledge of the region's vegetation, but also someone with lots of drive and enthusiasm to do justice to one of this country's floristic kingdoms. Jo Onderstall fits this description perfectly. She has all the qualifications and more . . . she even took the photographs herself!

Influenced and encouraged by her mother, who was a chairwoman of the Drakensberg and Eastern Free State branch of the Botanical Society for several years, Jo became acquainted with the South African flora at a very young age, and occasionally even carried off the prizes at flower shows. After matriculating at Harrismith, she qualified in Bloemfontein as a teacher in physical education, which is probably why she still puts such a premium on fitness. In 1950 she married Dr. Bill Onderstall, a doctor/farmer. Shortly afterwards they settled in Nelspruit where, for the first time, she got to know the beauty of the Lowveld scenery. Her interest in, and knowledge of photography began 34 years ago when she received a camera from her husband as a wedding present.

It stands to reason that Jo became involved with plants and gardens very early in her life. Not surprisingly, she was one of the founder members of the Lowveld branch of the Botanical Society, and I know that she is still one of its most active members. For many years she was involved in its management, amongst others as chairwoman. This led to her continued involvement in the Lowveld Botanic Garden since it was first established. Her love for, and knowledge of the indigenous vegetation of the area not only find expression in the decoration and maintenance of her own garden, but also in numerous lectures and publications. For readers of magazines such as "Garden and Home", "S.A. Panorama" and "Veld en Flora" she will be an old acquaintance. She is, moreover, an active member of the Tree and Wildlife societies.

A visit to "Ehlatini", the Onderstall's small farm among the wooded hills just outside Nelspruit, is an unforgettable experience.

Apart from its being a totally unspoilt sliver of the Lowveld where the silence sings in one's ears and one can truly find peace for one's soul, there is the added charm of a ritual enacted daily when birds and bushveld squirrels literally eat out of Jo's hand. Being privileged to have shared such a moment with Jo, I am convinced that she would like this book not only to be a source of scientific information, but also an instrument which will serve to bring its readers to a greater appreciation of nature.

I regard it as a privilege to contribute to the book in this way, and I would like to thank Jo Onderstall on behalf of all its prospective users.

PIET VAN WYK
Pretoria, April 1984

The lichen Old man's beard *(Usnea* sp.) dramatically draped over some branches.

Introduction

There is a hint of magic about the Transvaal Lowveld and Escarpment. It casts a spell which conjures up distinct images for different people.

For the tourist, for whom the Lowveld starts at the Escarpment, it means trout fishing in sparkling mountain streams; hiking along one of the trails and revelling in the scenery and bracing air; holidaying in the Kruger National Park or one of the many private nature reserves; a sunny, warm interlude in the heart of winter.

For those fortunate enough to live here it means having Heuglin's Robins at their bird baths, Purple-crested Louries and Trumpeter Hornbills eating their wild figs, squirrels scurrying around their gardens and bushbuck or duiker occasionally eating their lilies. It also means having dombeyas and erythrinas on the rocky outcrops and Barberton daisies growing wild around them. Perhaps the artists understand the magic better than others, for they find endless inspiration in the infinite variety of nature.

Running through, and embellishing the tapestry of the Lowveld and Escarpment's history, there is a thread of pure, bright gold. Throughout the ages the allure of gold has brought about turbulent change and this area was no exception. The romantic history of Pilgrim's Rest and Barberton has provided much exciting material for historians. Even before the advent of the white man, this mineral-rich region was being exploited, attested by the ancient copper-smelting ovens near Phalaborwa. Various minerals are still being mined and there is much to interest geologists in this region. Radiometric dating has shown that some of the oldest known rocks in the world occur in the southern Lowveld, where traces of primitive forms of life are preserved in ancient sedimentary rocks.

The most striking physical feature of the area dealt with in this guide is the majestic Drakensberg Escarpment. It runs roughly north to south and forms the western boundary of the region. The land drops sharply from the mountains into the foothills, with the steep slopes gradually easing off eastwards to the low-lying bush-clad plains that constitute the true Lowveld and which are punctuated with impressive rocky outcrops. The eastern limit is the Transvaal border with Moçambique. The northern limit is the Limpopo River and the area extends southwards to the border of Swaziland.

The region is fed by east-flowing rivers, some perennial, of which the major ones are the Limpopo, Olifants and Crocodile Rivers. It is a summer-rainfall region with precipitation occurring mainly in the form of sharp thundershowers. The mean annual rainfall varies from about 350 mm in the north-east to over 1 600 mm at places on the Escarpment. Proximity to the Tropic of Capricorn and the warm Moçambique current of the Indian Ocean, results in a sub-tropical climate in the low-lying areas. The Lowveld is virtually frost-free; with frost occurring infrequently only in specific areas. Cold winters with heavy frosts and occasional snowfalls are experienced on the Escarpment, which is often cloaked in mist.

VEGETATION

The vegetation of the Lowveld and Escarpment shows great diversity, ranging from scrubby, arid bush with poor grass cover, to beautiful woodland with tall, luxuriant grass, to moist evergreen forest. The Transvaal Lowveld is part of the southernmost portion of the great East African Plain, and because it is warm and relatively frost-free, many of the Lowveld's plants are tropical in affinity. The Drakensberg is part of a chain of mountains ex-

Previous page: A landmark of this region: the Three Rondavels at Blyde River Canyon.
◄ A striking landmark: Bourke's Luck Potholes.

Mountain grassland at Pilgrim's Rest.

tending northwards from the Cape, and certain Fynbos elements are evident along the Escarpment.

Although this is primarily a wild flower guide, in the main the trees have been used to indicate regions, as they are conspicuous and relatively easy to identify.

1. The Escarpment

The grandeur of the Drakensberg Escarpment is scenically unrivalled in the Transvaal: Blyde River Canyon with Mariepskop and the Three Rondavels, Bourke's Luck Potholes, God's Window, The Pinnacle, Graskop Gorge and Kaapsche Hoop, with delightful waterfalls tucked away in the folds of the mountains. There are breaks in the range, for example where the Olifants and Crocodile Rivers flow through from the west, but elsewhere the altitude is in excess of 1 500 m above sea level. The rainfall is high, ranging from about 900 mm to over 1 600 mm per annum. This area can be divided into grassland and forest regions.

(a) *Grassland:* These mountain grasslands contain a rich diversity of species such as androcymbiums and aristeas, red-hot pokers and pineapple lilies, scillas and ledebourias, gladioli and watsonias, brunsvigias, xysmalobiums and other asclepiads, crassulas galore, a wealth of terrestrial orchids and some of the summer-rainfall proteas. During the summer months these lush grasslands, especially the vleis with their rich carpet of flowers, are a delight to behold. The grassland is scattered with outcrops of weathered, lichen-covered rocks, often strangely and wonderfully shaped.

18

Rocky grassland on the Escarpment.

(b) *Forest:* There are very few large patches of true montane forest left on the Escarpment: Grootbosch near Tzaneen, the Mount Sheba Nature Reserve near Pilgrim's Rest and "Fairyland" near Graskop are perhaps the best-known examples. So many species of trees are represented that it is impossible to enumerate them, but a few of the more important are Cape Beech, Lemon Wood, Forest Waterwood, and the True Yellowwood (*Podocarpus latifolius*, p. 28). Transvaal Stinkwood and Green Witch-hazel are rare and localised. The forest floor is soft and spongy, rich in ferns, mosses and *Selaginella*. The moss-clad rocks are ideal habitats for various species of *Streptocarpus* and enchanting little terrestrial orchids, while the trees are often festooned with epiphytic orchids, ferns, mosses, old-man's-beard and other lichens.

2. The Foothills

This area comprises the eastern outlier of the Soutpansberg range, the eastern slopes of the Drakensberg and the mountains around Nelspruit and Barberton. It is in fact a transition zone linking the Escarpment to the plains and the vegetation is thus of a rather mixed nature. The altitude ranges from approximately 600 m to about 1 500 m and the mean annual rainfall varies from 500 mm to around 900 mm.

In some places the evergreen forest spills down as an extension from the mountains into densely wooded ravines. The remaining areas are woodland or open parkland with beautiful "specimen" trees: characteristic are Kiaat (*Pterocarpus angolensis*, p. 114), Natal Mahogany (*Trichilia emetica*, p. 122), Broad-leaved Boekenhout (*Faurea speciosa*, p. 84), False Kiaat (*Albi-*

19

zia versicolor, p. 98), Sickle Bush *Dichrostachys cinerea* subsp. *nyassana*, p. 102), and many more. As the foothills merge with the Lowveld massive granite outcrops, often dome-shaped can be seen. On some of these, in the south, isolated colonies of Kudu Lily (*Pachypodium saundersii*, p. 152) are occasionally found, generally on the drier northern or north-eastern aspects.

Some of the largest commercial timber plantations in the Republic are found on the Escarpment and foothills, and are of major economic importance to the region. Pines, gums and other alien trees have escaped from some of these plantations and it is imperative to protect the dwindling remnants of local indigenous forests from these invaders.

3. The Lowveld

The Lowveld comprises the low-lying plains between the foothills of the Drakensberg and the eastern boundary. The altitude ranges from about 150 m to 600 m above sea level and the average rainfall varies from 350 mm to 600 mm per annum. The long summer months can be oppressively hot and they are followed by brief mild winters that could pass for autumn elsewhere. There is a complex variation in vegetation as a result of the interaction between climate, topography and soil types. It could be subdivided into well over 30 types, but for the sake of simplicity, these are condensed to only two — namely the Lowveld as a whole and the riverine forests.

(a) *Lowveld:* There is a wealth of trees represented here, with no species being clearly dominant, except in a few specific areas. On rocky outcrops, in valleys and on sandy soils the bush becomes very dense while, generally speaking, it becomes drier towards the north and east. Most of the species are fairly common but a few are rare or localised, such as the endemic Lowveld Chestnut (*Sterculia murex*, p. 132), which grows on granite hills only in the south. On sandy to gritty soils there are often dense stands of terminalias and combretums, while tree euphorbias, such as *Euphorbia ingens* and *E. cooperi* (p. 126), often occur in colonies on granite faces. In a broad north-south belt in the east there is a predominance of Marula, Knobthorn (*Acacia nigrescens*, p. 100) and, to a lesser degree, Leadwood (*Combretum imberbe*, p. 140). The Umbrella Thorn (*Acacia tortilis* subsp. *heteracantha*, p. 102) is common in the central western region and towards the north Mopane becomes one of the dominant species, with pure stands in places. On some of the heavier soils it is of a short scrubby nature but towards Punda Maria it becomes a beautiful tree with lovely warm tints in autumn and winter. Although the Baobab (*Adansonia digitata*, p. 128) is widely distributed within the northern sector, it is not plentiful anywhere, except in a few colonies on rocky sites between Punda Maria and Pafuri.

In the north-east there are a few large patches of deep, well-drained sand, each with its own unique character, geologically and floristically. They are thought to be a link with the sands of the Kalahari and the Moçambique coastal plain. The vegetation is an intriguing mixture of elements from the Lowveld, the central Transvaal Bushveld and tropical Africa. A few of the interesting trees which occur here are the Propeller Tree, Mountain Mahogany, Round-leaved Saucer-berry, Fever Pod, and Toad Tree (*Tabernaemontana elegans*, p. 150).

One of the most beautiful flowering plants of the Lowveld is the succulent Impala Lily (*Adenium multiflorum*, p. 152) which flowers in winter. The Summer Impala Lily (*Adenium swazicum*, p. 152) is smaller but has equally lovely flowers. *Ornithogalum seineri* (p. 46) often occurs in attractive large stands. In early spring the watercourses of the Lowveld are ablaze with the brilliant scarlet flowers of the Flame Creeper (*Combretum microphyllum*, p. 140).

(b) *Riverine Forest:* Throughout the Lowveld there are narrow green belts of forest along the main rivers, which consist of large trees with dense undergrowth and creepers. They are conspicuous from a high vantage point and are particularly striking where they pass through

Umbrella thorn *(Acacia tortilis)*: dry Lowveld in western Kruger National Park.

Domed granite outcrop framed by Paperbark thorn *(Acacia sieberana* var. *woodii)*, near Nelspruit.

the arid regions. Some of the more common trees are the Sycamore Fig *(Ficus sycomorus*, p. 80), Matumi, Quinine Tree, Natal Mahogany *(Trichilia emetica*, p. 122), Fever Tree *(Acacia xanthophloea*, p. 102) and Wild Date Palm *(Phoenix reclinata*, p. 30).

For many people the Lowveld is synonymous with "the game reserve": the land of the lion, elephant and sable; giraffe, zebra and wildebeest. We trust that this guide will help them to see more in the Lowveld than only the fauna, and to become more aware and appreciative of the flora of this interesting region.

The snowy-white inflorescences of *Gerbera* sp.

The species illustrated in this guide:
Think of the Cape Peninsula and you picture fynbos with heath and proteas; think of Nama-
qualand and you imagine a great sea of brilliant spring colour; think of the Lowveld and the
Escarpment in general and the image that comes to mind is one of bush, trees and mountains, in places perennially green. In this guide therefore, you will find illustrated not only
the "flowers" but also the shrubs, trees and climbers. Some are conspicuous or common
while others are small or rare but equally interesting and beautiful. The Transvaal Lowveld
and Escarpment is a vast area with a rich and varied flora, so the guide must serve as an introduction, as it cannot be comprehensive.

A few introduced plants are included and they are clearly marked thus: ♦. They have become naturalised and constitute a grave threat to the indigenous flora e.g. the ubiquitous
Lantana (*Lantana camara*, p. 166), and Sesbania (*Sesbania punicea*, p. 110) which have established a firm foothold in the Lowveld, and the Water Hyacinth (*Eichhornia crassipes*, p. 34)
which infests some of the local rivers. Even the Jacaranda (*Jacaranda mimosifolia*, p. 178)

which is a popular and beautiful tree, is posing problems along some of the southern rivers. These plants are invasive and every attempt must be made to eradicate them completely.

How to use this guide

The illustrations and descriptions will help you in identifying the plants. It is sometimes difficult to obtain adequate photographs of tall and lanky plants, and in these cases the inflorescence only has been shown so as to provide maximum detail of the flowers. Distribution is based on specimens in the National Herbarium in Pretoria and the use of place names is not intended to indicate an exact locality but rather a district or an area. The approximate flowering times are given but these, as well as plant measurements, may vary according to climatic conditions and habitat. The flowering period may be brief, perhaps lasting for only 1–2 weeks, within the stated flowering times. The approximate altitudes at which plants occur are indicated as follows:

low up to 600 m above sea level   medium 600–1 500 m above sea level
high over 1 500 m above sea level

The roots of the Wild Fig *(Ficus sonderi)*.

Due to taxonomic revisions the botanical names of some plants have been changed. Only the commonly used synonyms have been included. If you know the plants by any other common names please write to the Botanical Society of South Africa, Kirstenbosch, Claremont, 7735 so that additional names may be incorporated in future editions.

Conservation of the region's floral heritage
The wild places in the Lowveld and on the great Escarpment where it is still possible to walk in the open veld or through a forest, were once lovelier and more plentiful. Magnificent trees have been chopped down which cannot be replaced in our lifetimes or those of our children, vast tracts of climax forest have been destroyed and rare plants have been removed from the veld, only to wither and die. Beautiful vistas have been ruined and previously clear streams have been polluted. Regularly every winter the veld and the bush are carelessly set ablaze, causing incalculable damage.

One wonders if the children of the next century will ever experience the heady, sweet perfume of Wild Jasmine, or marvel at the stuning flowers of the Scarlet River Lily? If each individual cared sufficiently to interest a few people, and show them that the natural heritage is not only ours, but also belongs to the future generations, then the destruction of the environment might be halted. We must care sufficiently, when contentious conservation issues arise, to make our protests heard. As responsible custodians we must conserve what remains, for if we fail in this, man himself will be the ultimate victim.

Protection of wild plants

Indigenous plants are protected by Ordinance 17 of 1967 which prohibits the picking of any indigenous plant within 300 feet of the centre of any public road, or the picking of any plant without the written permission of the landowner, or the picking of any plants that are proclaimed rare, endangered or protected, without the necessary permits. In this context "pick" also means to collect, cut off, chop down, uproot, damage or destroy and the prohibition pertains to every part of the plant. Applications for permits must be directed to the Director, Transvaal Provincial Department of Nature Conservation, Private Bag X209, Pretoria, 0001.

Many members of the Botanical Society of South Africa enjoy the privilege of growing these plants in their gardens. Seed of about 800 species is available annually to members. Indigenous plants are available from some nurseries including the National Parks Board nursery at Skukuza, and Botanical Society sales are held regularly.

Further information may be obtained from the following:

The Botanical Society of South Africa, Kirstenbosch, Claremont, 7735.

The Curator, Lowveld Botanic Garden, P.O. Box 1024, Nelspruit, 1200.

Where to find the flowers and obtain Permits

This area is well endowed with reserves and parks where the flowers illustrated in the text may be seen. In order to view flowers on private property, permission from the owner must be obtained. For specific information about these areas and any permits which may be required, please contact the following:

Transvaal Provincial Department of Nature Conservation, Private Bag X209, Pretoria, 0001.

Regional Director, Directorate of Forestry, Private Bag X11201, Nelspruit, 1200.

National Tourist Bureau, P.O. Box 679, Nelspruit, 1200.

National Parks Board, P.O. Box 787, Pretoria, 0001.

Publicity Office, Nelspruit Municipality, P.O. Box 45, Nelspruit, 1200.

Head Office, Board for Public Resorts, Private Bag X182, Pretoria, 0001.

CYATHEACEAE

Cyathea dregei (=Alsophila dregei) Tree Fern, Boomvaring

This perennial is a striking feature of the escarpment, and is also a highly prized horticultural subject which will thrive in a well-planned water garden. It is usually about 3 m high with a sturdy trunk and has a crown of graceful, arching fronds which are compound, with a firm, hard texture and are about 1,5 m long. Young, developing fronds, as well as the bases of mature fronds, are covered with tawny, woolly hairs. It grows gregariously along the banks of streams and forest margins and in ravines in the high rainfall areas of the escarpment and foothills.

PODOCARPACEAE

Podocarpus latifolius True Yellowwood, Opregte Geelhout

This is the National Tree of South Africa, the wood of which has been prized and extensively exploited since pioneer days, and is also a popular garden subject. It is about 4 m high in exposed places but about 20 m high in forests, where it may tower out above the canopy. The narrow, blue-green or dark green leaves are about 90 mm long. The male tree bears small, pink, elongated cones and the female tree bears blue to purple seeds on a fleshy, red receptacle. It grows in evergreen forest along the whole escarpment and *P. falcatus*, the Outeniqua Yellowwood, also occurs in this area.

ZAMIACEAE

Cycads, which fall under this family, are primitive plants and are, today, collectors' items. They enjoy special protection by law and the mere possession of a cycad requires a special permit in the Transvaal. The name Broodboom ("bread tree"), is derived from the fact that the pith in the stems of some cycads yields an edible starch.

Encephalartos laevifolius Kaapsche Hoop Cycad, Kaapsche Hoop Broodboom

This cycad, 2–4 m high, has grey-green pinnate leaves about 1 m long, with keeled leaflets and bears 1–5 conspicuous cones, male and female on separate trees. Commercial afforestation has taken its toll of this species, with only remnant populations surviving, mainly on the southern escarpment. This endangered species is carefully protected in the Starvation Creek Nature Reserve situated in Berlin State Forest.

Encephalartos transvenosus Modjadji Cycad, Modjadjibroodboom

The popular name refers to Modjadji, Rain Queen of the Lovedu, near whose kraal in the vicinity of Duiwelskloof, there is a forest of these trees: the only cycad forest in South Africa. Generally 5–13 m high, it has pinnate leaves about 2 m long, with glossy green leaflets which have a few sharp teeth. Male and female cones are produced on separate trees. These striking cycads have enjoyed protection by successive Rain Queens and in 1938 this unique forest was proclaimed a National Monument.

Previous page: The golden inflorescences of the Weeping Wattle *(Peltophorum africanum)*.

Cyathea dregei (=Alsophila dregei)

Podocarpus latifolius

Encephalartos laevifolius

Encephalartos transvenosus

ARECACEAE (=PALMAE)

Phoenix reclinata Wild Date Palm, Wildedadel

This palm, a common feature along river banks in the Lowveld, is related to the commercial date palm, having small edible fruits but with very little flesh. Usually 3–4 m high, it has pinnate leaves with sharply keeled leaflets. Tiny cream flowers are borne from August to October and the female tree produces small yellow dates. This tree is extensively utilised in tribal communities: the sap is used for making liquor, the crown-heart is eaten as a vegetable and the leaves provide material for hats, mats and brooms. Recorded from north to south in the low-lying areas.

Hyphaene natalensis (=H. crinita) Ilala Palm, Fan Palm, Lalapalm

Well-known to tourists in the northern sector of the Kruger National Park, this palm has distinctively arched, fan-shaped leaves. It is normally 2–4 m high and sometimes forms dense colonies. The long, pendent inflorescence bears flowers during September and October, the female tree subsequently producing pear-shaped fruits, the hard kernels of which are known as vegetable ivory. The tree is utilised in much the same way as *Phoenix reclinata*. Usually found not far from water, it is common in the northern Lowveld.

POACEAE (=GRAMINEAE)

This vast family of flowering plants includes grasses and reeds.

Phragmites mauritianus Reed, Dekriet, Fluitjiesriet

In autumn and early winter the vleis in this region are transformed into great seas of soft plumes waving in the breezes. These dense reedbeds are a haven for many bird species such as weavers and widow-birds. Robust and about 2 m high, this reed has greyish leaves with razor-sharp margins. The large, soft inflorescence is up to 450 mm long, with masses of tiny, silky, mauve-brown florets. Flowering period is from February to July and it has been recorded from north to south mainly at low to medium altitudes.

TYPHACEAE

Typha capensis (=T. latifolia subsp. *capensis)* Bulrush, Papkuil, Palmiet

Another well-known, gregarious vlei plant, the bulrush is distinguished by its striking, erect, brown inflorescence, conspicuous in midsummer. It is about 1,5 m high, with narrow leaves about 1 m long. The dark brown, velvety inflorescence consists of minute, densely packed flowers, male in the upper zone, female below and, when mature, it "explodes" into a mass of tiny, fluffy seeds. Recorded from the central and southern regions, at various altitudes.

Phoenix reclinata

Hyphaene natalensis (=H. crinita)

Phragmites mauritianus

Typha capensis (=T. latifolia subsp. *capensis)*

CYPERACEAE

Most of the plants in this family are known as sedges or "biesies" and are generally associated with vleis or damp grassland. The inflorescence consists of flower-bearing spikelets of various shapes and sizes, below which are usually a number of leaf-like bracts of varying sizes. There are numerous genera, only one of which is featured here.

Cyperus obtusiflorus var. *obtusiflorus* Sedge, Biesie, Wituintjie

This striking sedge is 200–600 mm high with very narrow leaves and bracts. The attractive, rounded inflorescence, 20 mm wide, has numerous, tightly packed, flattened, white spikelets with minute yellow flowers. Flowering takes place from October to February. It has been recorded at various altitudes throughout the whole area. *C. obtusiflorus* var. *flavissimus* is very similar but has brilliant yellow, shiny spikelets and is normally slightly smaller and less robust.

Cyperus immensus Sedge, Biesie

Aptly named, this handsome plant is probably the largest of the Lowveld sedges. It is extremely robust and attains a height of 2 m. The stiff stems are distinctly triangular, with sharp edges, and the hard leaves are up to 2 m long. The showy inflorescence is up to 200 mm wide with densely massed, light brown spikelets. Flowering occurs in midsummer. This immense sedge forms colonies and has been recorded from the central and southern mountains and foothills.

Cyperus distans Sedge, Biesie

This robust perennial, about 700 mm high, forms attractive clumps and has sharply triangular stems and narrow leaves about 500 mm long. The spreading inflorescence, about 200 mm wide, is repeatedly branched and has slender, golden-brown spikelets and rough, relatively broad bracts. Flowering takes place throughout the summer. Recorded at various altitudes from the central and southern regions.

Cyperus rupestris Sedge, Biesie

An attractive, gregarious little sedge 150–300 mm high with very slender leaves and thread-like bracts. The pretty inflorescence is a dense, radiating cluster of narrow, chocolate-brown spikelets that are up to 20 mm long. Flowering takes place in midsummer. The roots intertwine to form dense mats on rocks or in crevices. It has been recorded at low to medium altitudes in the central and southern districts.

Cyperus obtusiflorus var. *obtusiflorus*

Cyperus immensus

Cyperus distans

Cyperus rupestris

ARACEAE

The arum family consists of perennials, some of which are popular in horticulture. The intriguing inflorescence has an erect spadix with minute, crowded flowers (male in the upper zone, female below), partially enclosed in a spathe which is sometimes attractively coloured.

Zantedeschia aethiopica Arum Lily, Jack-in-the-pulpit, Aronskelk, Varkoorlelie

This soft, luxuriant plant is an excellent garden subject and is up to 1,5 m high. The leaf blade, about 300 mm long, is roughly triangular, with a deeply lobed base and tapering tip. The elegant inflorescence has an open, cream or white spathe which encircles the creamy-yellow spadix. Flowering occurs from October to December. It is a rare privilege to see this flower growing wild in this area. It has been recorded from a mere handful of localities along the escarpment, where it grows in open, wet situations.

Zantedeschia rehmannii Purple Arum, Pink Arum, Persvarkoor

One feature which distinguishes this lovely arum from the other species in the genus, is the fact that the leaf base is tapered and not lobed. The blade is up to 400 mm long, on a fleshy petiole. The spathe ranges from white, through shades of pink to deep maroon and encloses the yellow spadix. Flowering generally takes place in midsummer. Rather rare, it has been recorded from scattered localities on the southern escarpment in damp, rocky grassland.

Gonatopus angustus

This rather rare, elusive little perennial grows in deep humus in forest shade. It has a large, partially exposed, horizontal rootstock and a single compound leaf, the blade of which is about 200 mm long. The inflorescence, about 120 mm high, has a faintly striped, cream spathe which partially covers the creamy-white spadix. Flowers during November and December. Recorded from only a few localities in the extreme south.

PONTEDERIACEAE

♦ *Eichhornia crassipes* Water Hyacinth, Waterhiasint
PROCLAIMED WEED

A free-floating or rooted aquatic perennial forming dense mats. It has long feathery roots, roundish leaves on thick, spongy petioles and striking blue or mauve flowers. Indigenous to South America, it was introduced into South Africa and has become a very real menace in many polluted dams and rivers, in some cases completely covering a watercourse. Because of its capacity for vigorous vegetative reproduction, a colony is capable of doubling its size within 2 weeks. At present its main distribution appears to be along the Crocodile and Letaba Rivers where its presence gives cause for concern.

Zantedeschia aethiopica

Zantedeschia rehmannii

Gonatopus angustus

Eichhornia crassipes

COMMELINACEAE

Commelina africana var. *africana*

A branched, hairy perennial with stems about 200 mm long and narrow leaves about 60 mm long, their bases sheathing the stems. The dainty, lemon-yellow flowers are enclosed in a folded, heart-shaped spathe. They have 2 showy, paddle-shaped petals and a third which is much smaller and transparent. Flowering occurs mainly from October to February. It grows in open or wooded grassland at various altitudes and is widely distributed over the entire area.

Commelina modesta Blouselblommetjie

The clear, heavenly blue flowers of this species are most attractive and conspicuous. It is a straggly, hairy perennial with a few slender stems up to 400 mm long and narrow leaves about 100 mm long. Seen from the side, the folded spathe, which encloses the flowers, looks almost like the head of a Blue Crane. The glistening flowers resemble those of the previous species, the main difference being in the colour. Flowering takes place during the summer months. Occurs in open or lightly wooded grassland at low to medium altitudes and has been recorded from north to south.

Cyanotis speciosa Wandering Jew, Wandelende Jood, Bloupoeierkwassie

This arresting plant is related to the Wandering Jew, a well-known garden plant. It is hairy and about 300 mm high with narrow leaves up to 200 mm long. The superb little powder-puff flowers are borne in tight clusters and have conspicuous, bright yellow anthers. Flower colour varies from palest blue or mauve to deep violet or magenta. Generally found in medium to high altitude grassland, it has been recorded from north to south, flowering in summer.

ERIOCAULACEAE

Eriocaulon dregei var. *sonderanum* Pipewort

A dainty aquatic perennial which will be a rewarding find for individuals who are observant and diligent in their search. It is 150–200 mm high and grows in dense clumps with closely intertwined roots and a basal rosette of leaves. The very slender stem bears a small, spherical head, about 5 mm in diameter, of minute greyish flowers, usually in midsummer. This unusual little plant always has its roots in shallow water and has been recorded around Nelspruit and Barberton.

Commelina africana var. *africana*

Commelina modesta

Cyanotis speciosa

Eriocaulon dregei var. *sonderanum*

LILIACEAE

Plants in this family usually have bulbs, corms or rhizomes and the flowers have six tepals or lobes.

Gloriosa superba var. *superba* Flame Lily, Yellow Flame Lily, Vlamlelie, Geelvlamlelie

A superb plant with brilliant yellow flowers. It has a long, slender stem which climbs into adjacent vegetation by means of elongated, twining leaf-tips. The magnificent, pendent flowers have narrow, undulate tepals up to 70 mm long, recurved upwards, and flowering occurs from November to March. All parts of this plant, below and above ground, are extremely poisonous and ingestion can be fatal. It is found in rocky, bushy places and has been recorded from the whole Lowveld region and the foothills. Another variety, var. *virescens*, has scarlet-and-yellow segments and is found in Natal, particularly along the coast.

Littonia modesta Christmas Bells, Geelklokkies

This soft, climbing perennial, with a slender stem, also climbs by means of leaf tendrils. The pendent, orange flowers, 20–25 mm long, have neat, oval tepals and open from November to January. Recorded along the whole escarpment, where it grows in forest shade.

Androcymbium melanthioides forma *striatum* Little-men-in-a-boat, Pyjama Flower, Moses-in-die-mandjie, Bobbejaanskoen

The tiny flowers, nestled amongst the pyjama-striped bracts of this enchanting flower, could well be imagined as little men in a boat. It grows up to 300 mm high and has slender, keeled leaves up to 300 mm long. Approximately 6 tiny green flowers with conspicuous yellow anthers, are partially obscured by numerous large, showy bracts, usually white with green veins. Flowering is from December to March. Grows in rock crevices or open grassland and has been recorded from the central and southern escarpment and foothills.

Anthericum angulicaule

A robust perennial 300–500 mm high with a woody, knobbly rhizome and ribbed leaves which are 200–300 mm long. The flowers are about 15 mm wide and the white tepals each have a greeny-brown stripe down the centre. The flowers are crowded but only 2 or 3 open at a time, generally from June to January. Recorded from the central and southern escarpment and foothills in rocky, open grassland.

Gloriosa superba var. *superba*

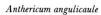

Littonia modesta

Androcymbium melanthioides forma *striatum*

Anthericum angulicaule

LILIACEAE

Red-hot pokers, which are so popular in gardens, are generally hybrids, but some of the wild plants are very beautiful and well worth cultivating.

Kniphofia linearifolia Poker, Vuurpyl

A distinctive feature of this *Kniphofia* is the neat, precise arrangement of the flowers, particularly evident when they are still in the bud stage. The keeled leaves are about 1 m long and the inflorescence, on a slender peduncle about 1,5 m high, has slender, tubular buds, pale to dull red, which open to yellow or yellow-green in late summer. Grows in grassland and marshes on the central and southern mountains and foothills.

Kniphofia multiflora Giant Poker, Reusevuurpyl

Because of its height, this *Kniphofia* is seldom confused with other species within this genus. It is up to 2 m high with soft, keeled leaves up to 1,5 m long. The narrow, cylindrical inflorescence has innumerable small, tubular flowers which are orange in bud, opening to yellow. Flowers briefly, within the period February to April. This rather rare plant forms spectacular colonies in vleis and on stream banks on the central and southern mountains and foothills.

Agapanthus is a solely South African genus of which the species as well as their hybrids are popular garden plants.

Agapanthus inapertus Drakensberg Agapanthus, Bloulelie

A most distinctive feature of the escarpment, it has beautiful, very dark blue flowers. It is about 1,5 m high with narrow, strap-shaped leaves and a cluster of pendent, tubular flowers. The deep blue to violet flower is 50–60 mm long with slightly spreading tepals. Flowering takes place from January to March. Grows on forest fringes and in grassland on the central and southern mountains.

Albuca setosa

This slender perennial, with its white flowers, is conspicuous in burnt veld. It is about 300 mm high, with a few narrow leaves approximately 300 mm long. The tepals are about 20 mm long, each with a central green stripe, the outer 3 spreading and the inner 3 more or less enclosing the pistil and stamens. Flowering is from July to September. Recorded from the mountains around Nelspruit, Kaapsche Hoop and Barberton, where it grows in open, rocky grassland.

Kniphofia linearifolia

Agapanthus inapertus

Kniphofia multiflora

Albuca setosa

LILIACEAE

Aloes are perennial succulents with leaves which are usually in the form of a rosette, having prickles on the margins. The tubular flowers are generally about 40 mm long, with 6 tepals. Indigenous and hybrid aloes are excellent subjects for well-planned succulent gardens.

Aloe arborescens Krantz Aloe, Kransaalwyn

The specific name *arborescens* means "becoming a tree" and is an apt description of this species' much-branched habit. It can attain a height of 3 m. There are 1–4 peduncles per leaf rosette, with coral-red flowers borne in conical inflorescences from May to July. It hybridises readily in the wild with a number of local species, and has been recorded along the central and southern escarpment and foothills. It is a colourful winter feature in rocky landscapes of places such as Kaapsche Hoop and "Fairyland", near Graskop.

Aloe barbertoniae Barberton Aloe, Barbertonse Aalwyn

This *Aloe* is generally stemless and about 1 m high. The leaves are green and reddish brown with pale, irregular markings and twisted, withered tips. The grey-mauve peduncle is branched, with lax inflorescences of coral-pink flowers which open from June to August. Recorded from only a few localities, viz. Tzaneen, Nelspruit and Barberton. Grows in open woodland and on rocky outcrops, generally in light shade.

Aloe boylei

An attractive summer-flowering *Aloe* which is usually stemless: the inflorescence is about 300 mm high. It has relatively thin, soft leaves with soft prickles along the white margins. The rather squat inflorescence has lemon, apricot or orange flowers with green-tipped tepals. Flowering takes place from December to January. It grows in open, moist, hilly grassland and has been recorded from Tzaneen southwards.

Aloe chortolirioides subsp. *chortolirioides*

This small, tufted *Aloe* forms striking, dense clumps high up in the mountains. About 250 mm high, it has woody, branched stems and narrow, linear leaves with minute teeth on the margins. The flowers are usually warm coral with yellow-green tips but occasional specimens have apricot coloured flowers. In recently burnt veld this aloe is a splendid sight and flowering takes place from May to September. It is confined to the southern mountains where it grows on rocky slopes. It is relatively rare and enjoys careful protection in the Tinie Louw Nature Reserve near Barberton.

Aloe arborescens

Aloe barbertoniae

Aloe boylei

Aloe chortolirioides subsp. *chortolirioides*

LILIACEAE

Aloe kniphofioides Grass Aloe, Grasaalwyn

Slender, erect and about 400 mm high, this inconspicuous, stemless *Aloe* is sometimes overlooked in the veld. The narrow leaves have minute teeth on the margins and the lax inflorescence has widely spaced coral to red flowers with yellow-green tips. Flowering is from August to November. It grows in the south, in medium to high altitude grassland.

Aloe marlothii Mountain Aloe, Bergaalwyn

This spectacular *Aloe* brightens the winter landscape with its magnificent candelabra of yellow to orange flowers. It is 2–6 m high and the stem is often clothed in old, dead leaves. The leaves have prickles on both surfaces as well as on the margins. Flowering takes place from June to August. It hybridises readily with other local species such as *A. arborescens, A. petricola, A. barbertoniae* and *A. sessiliflora*. Found on rocky outcrops and mountain slopes, it has been recorded from the central and southern regions.

Aloe petricola Rock Aloe, Rotsaalwyn

Petricola, which means "inhabiting rocky places", is a most appropriate name for this *Aloe*. It is stemless and up to 1 m high when in flower. The leaves occasionally have prickles on the blades as well as the margins. The inflorescences have an interesting bi-coloured effect: greenish white to red, or yellow to orange, but uniform orange colouring also occurs. During July and August this *Aloe* provides a bright splash of colour against the grey rocks. It hybridises with some local species and has been recorded on the mountains and foothills, from Sabie southwards.

Aloe sessiliflora Lebombo Aloe, Lebombo-aalwyn

This *Aloe* grows up to 2 m high when in flower with a single or branched stem which may be erect or procumbent. The leaves, relatively narrow, are normally pale green but become brick-red in dry, exposed situations. Each rosette bears 1–5 slender inflorescences with very short, yellow flowers which have conspicuous orange anthers and contain copious amounts of thick, dark red nectar, much favoured by birds and bees. Flowering occurs during July and August. Found in bushy or rocky places over a wide range of altitudes. Recorded from scattered localities in the central and southern regions.

Aloe kniphofioides

Aloe marlothii

Aloe petricola

Aloe sessiliflora

LILIACEAE
Dipcadi viride
It is very easy to overlook this slender, grass-like perennial in the veld. It is up to 500 mm high with 2–4 narrow, keeled, basal leaves about 300 mm long. The small, tubular, green flowers are widely spaced and the 3 outer tepals bear long appendages which are strongly reflexed when the flowers are fully open. Flowering takes place from November to January. Recorded from the central and southern areas in open, rocky grassland at medium to high altitudes.

Ledebouria floribunda
A soft, fleshy plant up to 500 mm high with a large bulb about 100 mm in diameter, and broad, tapering leaves with irregular purple blotches. The peduncle is often gracefully curved and bears masses of tiny cream-and-green flowers with reflexed tepals and protruding stamens and styles. Each bulb bears 2–4 inflorescences and flowering takes place from October to December. It grows on rocky outcrops at low to medium altitudes and has been recorded in the south.

Ornithogalum saundersii Transvaal Chinkerinchee, Transvaalse Tjienkerientjee

This beautiful chinkerinchee, with its attractive flowers, may look innocuous but it is very poisonous to certain animals. It is 1–1,5 m high and has soft, strap-shaped leaves about 600 mm long. The inflorescence, which is initially rounded, elongates during flowering. Each white flower, which is about 25 mm wide, has spreading tepals and a conspicuous bottle-green ovary. Flowering takes place during January and February. It forms little colonies on rocky outcrops in the southern areas.

Ornithogalum seineri
Much smaller than the previous species, this little *Ornithogalum* grows about 300 mm high and has slender leaves. The pretty inflorescence is round or pyramidal, with a little terminal tuft of narrow bracts. The flowers, which are about 15 mm wide, have white tepals, each with a pale green stripe down the centre. Flowering takes place during October and November. Recorded from the central and southern Lowveld where it forms spectacular colonies in open, dry grassland.

Dipcadi viride

Ledebouria floribunda (Scilla floribunda)

Ornithogalum saundersii

Ornithogalum seineri

LILIACEAE

Scilla natalensis Blue Squill, Blue Scilla, Blouberglelie

This charming perennial has dainty little flowers varying from pale, powder-blue to dark blue. It grows up to 1 m high and the erect, basal leaves, which vary from being smooth to being covered with rough hairs, are up to 400 mm long. Although there are numerous flowers, only a few open at a time, mainly during September and October. Blue Squill forms colonies in damp grassland on the central and southern escarpment.

Scilla nervosa

In contrast to the previous species, this *Scilla* has snow-white to greenish flowers. It is a robust plant, up to 400 mm high when in flower and has basal leaves that taper to a sharp point, with thick margins and conspicuously raised veins. Flowering takes place from September to December. Recorded in grassland from the central and southern mountains.

Eucomis autumnalis subsp. *clavata (=E. undulata)* Pineapple Lily, Wildepynappel, Pynappellelie

This striking perennial does, indeed, resemble a pineapple and is grown with great success in gardens. It grows up to 300 mm high and has soft, fleshy, basal leaves with crisped, undulate margins. The inflorescence has pale green flowers topped with a conspicuous tuft of bracts. Flowering takes place from February to early April. The swollen green fruits are approximately triangular. Found in open or lightly shaded grassland on the central and southern escarpment and foothills.

Eucomis comosa var. *pole-evansii (=E. pallidiflora)* Pineapple Lily, Wildepynappel, Pynappellelie

In most respects this perennial is larger, more robust and more spectacular than the previous species, attaining a height of 1,2 m. The flowers are cream or pale green and the tuft of terminal bracts is relatively small. Flowering takes place from January to March. Confined to a few localities on the southern escarpment where it grows in marshes and vleis, forming large colonies.

Scilla natalensis

Scilla nervosa

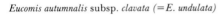
Eucomis autumnalis subsp. *clavata (=E. undulata)*

Eucomis comosa var. *pole-evansii (=E. pallidiflora)*

LILIACEAE

Dracaena hookeriana Large-leaved Dragon Tree, Grootblaardrakeboom

This handsome evergreen plant makes a dramatic garden subject. It is 2–4 m high with a large rosette of broad, tapering leaves up to 600 mm long. The showy, much-branched inflorescence has numerous single or clustered, shiny-white flowers which open during December and January. The fruits, round orange berries, are eaten greedily by birds. Found in high altitude, open forest, this *Dracaena* has been recorded from scattered localities from north to south.

Sansevieria hyacinthoides (=S. guineensis) Mother-in-law's Tongue, Skoonma-se-tong

The common name probably refers to the hard texture and sharp edges of the leaves of this plant! Capable of forming dense colonies, it has an extremely vigorous rhizome and grows up to 450 mm high. The fibrous leaves have pale- and dark-green marbling and red margins. The dense inflorescence has fragrant, shiny-white flowers which open from January to March. The bright orange fruit is knobbly and 3-lobed. The leaf fibre is sometimes used for rope-making and Spectacled Weavers have been seen to strip off the fibre for nest-making. Often associated with granite outcrops, it has been recorded from the central and southern regions at various altitudes.

Protasparagus angusticladus (=Asparagus aethiopicus var. *angusticladus)* Wild Asparagus, Wildeaspersie

Recently revised, the genus *Asparagus* has been split into 2 genera, viz. *Asparagus*, to which the edible species belongs, and *Protasparagus*, to which the African species belong. The plant featured here is a robust, prickly scrambler with tiny narrow leaves borne in little clusters and strong, curved prickles. Clouds of minute, creamy-white flowers adorn the bush during August and September but it would seem as though flowering does not take place every year. The fruit is a small red berry. Recorded in the south where it grows in sandy, rocky places.

Smilax kraussiana Wag-'n-bietjie-klimop

This viciously armed climber would adequately suffice as poor man's barbed wire! The extremely vigorous, tough stems have paired tendrils for purchase and small, but strong, hooked prickles. The blue-green leaves are oval and the inflorescence, 20–25 mm in diameter, is a spherical cluster of tiny, creamy-green flowers. The flowering period is from December to April. Female plants produce attractive clusters of small purple berries, like bunches of miniature grapes. Common in bushy areas and forest margins on the central and southern mountains and foothills.

Dracaena hookeriana

Sanseviera hyacinthoides (=S. guineensis)

Protasparagus angusticladus (=Asparagus aethiopicus var. *angusticladus)*

Smilax kraussiana

AMARYLLIDACEAE

Haemanthus hirsutus Velskoenblaar

Fortunately there are places where this beautiful perennial can still be seen in its natural habitat. It grows 200–300 mm high and has 2 broad, oval leaves, smooth above and hairy below. The inflorescence consists of massed white flowers, ageing to a delicate pink, with protruding stamens and styles. Flowering takes place from November to March, followed by fleshy red berries. Recorded from the southern mountains and foothills, where it grows in grassland, often peeping out of rock crevices.

Scadoxus multiflorus subsp. *multiflorus (=Haemanthus sacculus)*

Seen flowering in the veld, this charming perennial has a singularly delicate beauty. It grows up to 300 mm high and has undulate leaves and a sturdy, maroon-spotted peduncle. The inflorescence is almost spherical, 100–150 mm in diameter, with warm-pink flowers which have slender, spreading tepals and protruding stamens and styles. Flowering takes place during October and November. The fruits are fleshy orange berries. Grows in light shade in open woodland and has been recorded from scattered localities in the central and southern Lowveld.

Scadoxus puniceus (=Haemanthus magnificus) Blood Lily, Paintbrush, Bloedlelie, Seerooglelie

Almost startling in its beauty, this perennial can have great impact in a garden, but is at its best in its natural habitat. It grows up to 500 mm high and has shiny undulate leaves and a maroon-spotted peduncle. The magnificent inflorescence, up to 150 mm wide, has red or maroon bracts surrounding densely massed small, dark orange to red flowers. Flowering takes place during October and November and buck are known to eat the whole inflorescence just before the flowers open, while the fleshy red berries are eaten by birds and squirrels. Scattered over the entire Lowveld-escarpment area, it grows in lightly shaded grassland or on sheltered rocky outcrops.

Boophane disticha Tumbleweed, Seerooglelie, Gifbol

This perennial has a spectacular inflorescence which trebles its size as it dries out, to become one of the so-called tumbleweeds so often seen against fences, blown there by the wind. It is very poisonous, grows 300–400 mm high and has greyish leaves which appear after the flowers. The spherical inflorescence, about 200 mm in diameter, has numerous pink flowers which open from September to November. Recorded at various altitudes throughout the whole area, in open grassland, but is not plentiful anywhere, despite its wide distribution.

Haemanthus hirsutus

Scadoxus multiflorus subsp. *multiflorus*
  (= *Haemanthus sacculus*)

Scadoxus puniceus (= *Haemanthus magnificus*)

Boophane disticha

AMARYLLIDACEAE

Clivia caulescens Clivia, Boslelie

This colourful forest perennial can become up to 1 m high when in flower and has dark green, strap-shaped leaves which are the perfect foil for the brilliant, dark orange to red, pendent flowers. The tepals have yellow-green tips. Flowering takes place from October to December. The fruits are large red berries. Recorded from the whole length of the escarpment, it grows in humus on the forest floor and occasionally as an epiphyte in the forks of trees, the seed probably having been deposited there by birds.

Clivia miniata Clivia, Boslelie

This handsome forest perennial is popular in horticulture. About 500 mm high, it has strap-shaped leaves and a showy, spreading cluster of orange to red flared flowers. Flowering takes place during September and October. The fruits are large red berries. Found in deep humus in full forest shade, it has been recorded only from the mountains near Barberton.

Brunsvigia natalensis Candelabra flower, Kandelaarblom

This attractive perennial is up to 500 mm high, with a large bulb up to 200 mm in diameter and 2–6 rough, strap-shaped leaves. The slender peduncle carries a beautiful inflorescence, about 300 mm wide, of crimson, trumpet-shaped flowers which open from November to January. The inflorescence doubles its size as it matures and dries out. Confined to the escarpment, it grows in open, swampy grassland and has been recorded from only a few localities around Mariepskop and Graskop. Its numbers seem to be on the decline and it should perhaps be added to the list of protected plants for the Transvaal.

Brunsvigia radulosa Candelabra flower

This is another tumbleweed, the dry inflorescence enlarging to a diameter of 700 mm. It has a bulb up to 200 mm in diameter, which is sometimes partially exposed, and broad, rough leaves which lie more or less flat on the ground. The stout peduncle is about 300 mm high and bears a striking inflorescence approximately 250 mm wide. The bright pink flowers have widely spreading tepals and open during January and February. This relatively rare plant has been recorded from only a few localities around Pilgrim's Rest and Barberton, in open, rocky grassland.

Clivia caulescens

Clivia miniata

Brunsvigia natalensis

Brunsvigia radulosa

AMARYLLIDACEAE

Crinum macowanii River Crinum, Rivierlelie

This splendid *Crinum* has a rosette of long, grey-green, strap-shaped leaves. The stout peduncle carries a graceful cluster of pendent, trumpet-shaped flowers each up to 200 mm long. They are white or palest pink, with darker keels and black horse-shoe anthers. Flowering is from October to December. The roundish, knobbly fruit is a thin-walled capsule containing large, irregularly shaped seeds. Found in a variety of habitats at various altitudes in the central and southern regions.

Cyrtanthus contractus Fire Lily, Vuurlelie

Perhaps the finest *Cyrtanthus* in this region, it provides a welcome splash of brilliant colour in bare or burnt veld. It has 2–3 narrow leaves of varying lengths and the maroon peduncle carries a cluster of about 6 pendent, scarlet flowers, each approximately 80 mm long. The long, slender tubular flower has spreading lobes. Flowering takes place during August and September. It is relatively rare and has been recorded from only a few localities in the extreme south, in medium to high altitude grassland.

Cyrtanthus galpinii Fire Lily, Vuurlelie

In some areas this delightful, dainty perennial is one of the first to flower after the veld has been burnt. It is about 150 mm high and has 1–2 narrow leaves which sometimes appear after the flowers. The trumpet-shaped flower is warm pink, salmon or orange, with a few darker stripes in the throat, and is about 40 mm wide. Flowering takes place from June to August. It grows in wooded, rocky situations and has been recorded only in the extreme south.

VELLOZIACEAE

Xerophyta retinervis (= *Vellozia retinervis*) Bobbejaanstert, Aapstert

A flower posy atop a monkey's tail sounds most improbable but this intriguing "phenomenon" may be witnessed every year after the first spring rains, when the apparently dead, lifeless stems of Bobbejaanstert burst into new life. The fibrous stems consist mainly of fire-proof layers of old leaf bases, this protection enabling the plants to survive the annual ravages of fire. In early spring the new leaves and pretty white, pink or mauve flowers appear. Normally associated with exposed granite outcrops at low to medium altitudes, it has been recorded throughout the Lowveld and on the foothills.

Crinum macowanii

Cyrtanthus contractus

Cyrtanthus galpinii

Xerophyta retinervis (= Vellozia retinervis)

HYPOXIDACEAE

Hypoxis obtusa

This soft, hairy perennial, 200–300 mm high, has basal, strap-shaped leaves which are deeply keeled, and shiny yellow flowers, the outer 3 segments of which are dark green and very hairy on the outside. The flowers are 20–30 mm wide and their vibrant colour brightens the veld between August and December. Recorded from scattered localities in the central and southern mountains in open, rocky grassland.

Hypoxis rooperi var. *rooperi*

The largest and showiest of the local species of *Hypoxis*, this shaggy perennial has arching, keeled leaves which are conspicuously and neatly arranged in 3 ranks. The brilliant yellow flowers are similar to those of the previous species but are about 50 mm wide. Flowering takes place from September to December. The strong, fibrous leaves are utilised in the making of binding material. Grows in open, rocky grassland at low to medium altitudes and has been widely recorded from north to south.

DIOSCOREACEAE

Dioscorea sylvatica Elephant's Foot, Wild Yam, Olifantsvoet

Related to *D. elephantipes*, the well-known Elephant's Foot, this perennial also has a large rootstock with an irregular woody surface and long, slender, twining stems. The willow-green, slightly fleshy leaves are broad and heart-shaped, and the lax inflorescences have minute, creamy-green flowers which open from November to January. The triangular fruits, containing flat seeds with thin papery wings, remain on the plant for some months. The rootstock contains *diosgenin*, which is used in the preparation of cortisone. This has led to over-exploitation, and in some districts of the Transvaal it has been virtually eradicated. Recorded from scattered localities from north to south, in bushy, rocky places at various altitudes.

Dioscorea quartiniana

This *Dioscorea* is also a climber with twining stems but the leaves differ from those of the previous species in that they are digitately compound, with 5 undulate leaflets about 50 mm long. The dense, pendent inflorescence is cylindrical with minute, fragrant ivory flowers which open from December to February. Fruits and seeds resemble those of the previous species, but the fruit is somewhat shorter and rather squat. Recorded from the central and southern areas, in low to medium altitude woodland.

Hypoxis obtusa

Hypoxis rooperi var. *rooperi*

Dioscorea sylvatica

Dioscorea quartiniana

IRIDACEAE

Aristea woodii

An attractive perennial, 400–600 mm high when in flower, with tapering leaves and an erect inflorescence of shimmering pale blue, mauve or white flowers which are 15–20 mm wide. Each bloom opens in the early morning and by noon it has twisted into a tight spiral, becoming inky-blue in colour. Flowering time is from December to February. Widely recorded along the entire escarpment and foothills, in open grassland or swampy areas.

Schizostylis coccinea Scarlet River Lily, Rooirivierlelie

The exquisite scarlet flowers of this water-loving perennial are most distinctive. The plant is about 500 mm high, with narrow leaves, and bears 6–10 glistening flowers, each 50–60 mm wide, with broad, spreading segments. Flowering time is from December to February. Found in marshes and along the banks of streams, and recorded from only a few localities on the central and southern escarpment. It seems to be disappearing from places to which the general public has access and may one day survive only in private sanctuaries and nature reserves.

Crocosmia aurea

An excellent garden subject, it could possibly be one of the parent plants of the popular Montbretia. About 700 mm high when in flower, it has slender leaves with prominent midribs and a branched inflorescence with bright orange, pendent flowers, each about 50 mm wide. They have spreading lobes and protruding stamens and styles. Flowering takes place during January and February. The attractive fruit is a knobbly orange capsule which splits open to reveal shiny purplish-black seeds, relished by birds. Usually found in forest shade on the central and southern escarpment.

Crocosmia paniculata (= Curtonus paniculatus) Waaierlelie

More robust than the previous species, it has long broad leaves that are conspicuously "pleated" lengthwise. The dark-red flowers have shorter lobes than *C. aurea* but also open during January and February. Large colonies are found in moist grassland on the southern escarpment.

Aristea woodii

Schizostylis coccinea

Crocosmia aurea

Crocosmia paniculata (= Curtonus paniculatus)

IRIDACEAE

The name *Gladiolus* means "little sword" and refers to the shape of the leaves. All species of Gladiolus are perennials with corms, grey-green leaves and flowers with 6 lobes. Most of the beautiful specimens grown in gardens and hothouses all over the world are hybrids.

Gladiolus dalenii (= G. natalensis and *G. psittacinus)*

This large perennial grows up to 1 m high, and the species is possibly one of the parent plants of the garden hybrids. The attractive flowers, each about 50 mm wide, are hooded and the colour varies from yellow-green to orange, sometimes streaked with maroon. Flowering usually takes place from December to April. Found in grassland and on rocky outcrops, mainly at medium to high altitudes and recorded from numerous localities from north to south.

Gladiolus ecklonii subsp. *ecklonii*

Depending on local conditions, this striking perennial can be anything from 300–600 mm high when in flower. The white or cream flowers, each about 50 mm long, have bold maroon speckling and are partially enclosed by large, conspicuous bracts. The flowering period is from January to March. It grows in grassland and on rocky slopes and has been recorded from the central and southern mountains and foothills. Besides the typical subspecies, two others are recognised.

Gladiolus hollandii

This gregarious *Gladiolus* is particularly beautiful because its flowers are borne in such abundance. The plant is generally 600–800 mm high and the pale pink flowers are liberally decorated with red or maroon speckles and streaks. The branched style and dark maroon anthers complete the delightful picture. Flowering takes place from February to April. Occurs in rocky grassland at medium altitudes, only in the south, where its delicate beauty enhances the landscape.

Gladiolus sericeo-villosus

This robust perennial reaches 2 m in height when in flower and has stiff leaves with prominent yellow ribs. The numerous, close-set flowers are neatly arranged on opposite sides of the axis and are usually a pale, dull mauve with faint yellow-green markings on the lower lobes. As the lobes do not spread, the flowers are relatively narrow, 15–20 mm wide. Flowering takes place from April to May. Rather rare, it has been recorded from only a few localities on the central and southern foothills, in wooded grassland.

Gladiolus dalenii (= G. natalensis, G. psittacinus)

Gladiolus ecklonii subsp. *ecklonii*

Gladiolus hollandii

Gladiolus sericeo-villosus

IRIDACEAE

Gladiolus varius var. *varius*

Bearing exquisite, clear pink flowers, this is one of the loveliest *Gladiolus* species. The flower is about 50 mm wide, the top lobe being conspicuously hooded and the 3 lower lobes having dark pink streaks. Flowering occurs between January and May. Tucked into rock crevices, it brightens the rocky landscape of the southern escarpment.

Gladiolus woodii

The subtle hues of its glowing flowers give this dainty *Gladiolus* an ethereal quality. It is generally about 400 mm high with flowers about 25 mm long. The upper 3 lobes are golden brown and the lower 3 yellow. Of the lower lobes, the laterals are folded and much smaller than the central, a feature which distinguishes this plant from the other species mentioned in the text. The flowering period is brief, occurring during October and November. Grows in grassland on the central and southern escarpment and foothills. There is also a colour form with purple and brown flowers.

Watsonia transvaalensis

In late summer and early autumn this handsome *Watsonia* graces the rolling mountain grassland of the central and southern escarpment, in places providing whole fields of colour. It grows up to about 1 m high when in flower and the leaves have prominent yellow ribs and margins. The pretty pink flowers have spreading lobes, each with a central dark pink stripe. It is one of the most plentiful watsonias in this area.

Watsonia watsonioides

The precise, neat arrangement of the flowers on opposite sides of the axis, makes this *Watsonia* most distinctive. It is a slender perennial, about 1 m high, with stiff leaves which have hard, prominent midribs and margins. The flowers are white or ivory, sometimes yellow, and the lobes, which do not spread out, are only slightly curved at the tips. Flowering time is late summer and early autumn. Grows in mountain grassland, only in the extreme south.

Gladiolus varius var. *varius*

Gladiolus woodii

Watsonia transvaalensis

Watsonia watsonioides

ZINGIBERACEAE

Siphonochilus aethiopicus (=Kaempferia aethiopica) Wild Ginger, Wildegemmer

Redolent of ginger and spices, the wild ginger has rhizomes that taste like those of the true ginger, to which it is related. It has a tuft of leaves which develop during or after flowering and the enchanting, fragrant flowers, which are pale pinky-mauve, appear at ground level. They are about 60–80 mm in diameter and, although each delicate bloom lasts but a day, a plant may produce up to 25 flowers. The flowering period is from October to December. Grows in clumps on wooded, rocky outcrops at low to medium altitudes in the central and southern regions. Rare and localised, its numbers are diminishing, possibly due to the fact that it is used medicinally: the rhizome is chewed to clear blocked nasal passages.

ORCHIDACEAE

Orchids have always fascinated man and this family is one of the largest and perhaps the most diversified in the plant kingdom. Orchids differ from other flowers in some respects, for example they usually have 3 sepals and 3 petals, with 1 petal, called the lip, differing markedly from the others in shape, size or colour; some orchids have 1 or 2 spurs attached to the dorsal sepal or the lip; the stamen and pistil are united into a column and the pollen grains are consolidated into masses called pollinia.

Cynorkis kassneriana

This small specimen is up to 250 mm high with a single basal leaf and pretty, mauve or pink flowers with short glandular hairs. The hooded, dorsal sepal is about 5 mm long and the 3-lobed lip has purple spots. The spur is short and slender. The flowering period is from February to March. It grows in the rich humus of indigenous and pine forests all along the escarpment.

Habenaria epipactidea

Finding this handsome perennial in the veld is always a lovely surprise. It is up to 500 mm high, with overlapping leaves and a dense inflorescence with cream-and-green flowers, of which the narrow lip is about 12 mm long. Flowering takes place during January and February. Rare in this area, it has been recorded only from the south, in medium altitude woodland.

Bonatea pulchella

This elusive, small species hides in shaded undergrowth and its flowers have a fragile, ethereal beauty. The sepals, of which the dorsal is hooded, are short and snow-white. The spur and the petal- and lip-lobes are thread-like and green-tipped. The spur, swollen towards the tip, is about 60 mm long. The flowers open in mid-winter. Recorded from the Nelspruit district, in rocky woodland.

Siphonochilus aethiopicus (=Kaempferia aethiopica)

Cynorkis kassneriana

Habenaria epipactidea

Bonatea pulchella

ORCHIDACEAE

Brachycorythis pleistophylla

This locally rare and beautiful orchid, known mainly from tropical Africa, was recently collected in the eastern Transvaal. It grows 250–800 mm high and has lanceolate leaves with red margins. The flowers are rose-pink to deep mauve, with white and yellow in the throat. The curved, bi-lobed lip, about 12 mm long, is conspicuously larger than the sepals and petals. Flowering takes place in January. It grows in mountain grassland near Pilgrim's Rest and Graskop.

Satyriums characteristically have twin spurs attached to the lip which is uppermost and hooded, while the sepals and petals are in some cases fused to the lip.

Satyrium hallackii subsp. *ocellatum (=S. ocellatum)*

This gregarious *Satyrium* grows up to 500 mm high with narrow, pointed leaves and numerous, close-set flowers which vary from white or palest pink to a rich watermelon-pink. They are 10–15 mm wide with spurs about 25 mm long. Colonies of this species thrive in damp grassland on the central and southern escarpment and foothills. Flowering takes place in summer, mainly from December to February.

Satyrium neglectum subsp. *neglectum*

This tall, slender *Satyrium* is up to 1 m high with 1–2 leaves on a short shoot. The sturdy flowering stem is separate and bears tiny, fragrant, bright pink flowers which are up to 10 mm wide, with spurs up to 20 mm long. The flowering period is between January and March. Recorded from a few localities on the southern escarpment, in grassland.

Satyrium trinerve

Conspicuous bracts amongst the neat, compact little flowers, are characteristic of this *Satyrium*. It is 200–800 mm high with 2–5 narrow leaves. The flowers are cream and yellow; and the spurs, hood and sepals are 3–4 mm long. Flowering takes place from December to January. Grows in marshes and damp grassland high up on the central and southern mountains.

Brachycorythis pleistophylla

Satyrium hallackii subsp. *ocellatum* (=*S. ocellatum*)

Satyrium neglectum subsp. *neglectum*

Satyrium trinerve

ORCHIDACEAE

Disa chrysostachya

Opening at about Christmas time, the colourful inflorescences of this *Disa* look like bright candles in the vleis where they grow. It is a slender plant, up to 1 m high with close-set flowers which are about 12 mm wide. The hooded sepal is yellow and the laterals salmon or orange, while the 2 small petals crossed over below the hood, and the small, narrow lip, are salmon. Recorded from the central and southern mountains.

Disa nervosa

A splendid, robust *Disa*, 400–800 mm high, it has narrow, clasping leaves and numerous bright pink flowers with narrow sepals and petals. The dorsal sepal is hooded, with a slender, horizontal spur about 15 mm long. The lateral sepals and very narrow lip are up to 20 mm long. This beautiful orchid flowers during January and February and grows in open grassland on the central and southern escarpment.

Disa stachyoides

Although not very large, this mountain orchid is most attractive. It is about 300 mm high with few leaves and a short inflorescence with mauve or purple flowers. The dorsal sepal is hooded and the laterals are oblong and concave, about 5 mm long. There are 2 tiny petals below the hood, the white lip is mauve-tipped and the broad, flat spur is about 5 mm long. Flowering takes place from November to January. It grows in mountain grassland and has been recorded from scattered localities on the central and southern escarpment.

Herschelia baurii Bloumoederkappie

This small species varies from sky-blue to deep mauve. It is 200–300 mm high with leaves that appear after flowering has taken place. The flower has a large, open, hooded sepal, a bearded lip and an up-tilted spur about 5 mm long. It flowers during September and October in mountain grassland and has been recorded from scattered localities in the central and southern regions.

Disa chrysostachya

Disa nervosa

Disa stachyoides

Herschelia baurii

ORCHIDACEAE

Liparis bowkeri (=L. neglecta)

Often hidden in the humus of the forest floor, this small, elusive orchid is only 100–150 mm high. It has exposed, fleshy, green pseudobulbs with soft, pleated leaves. The slender stem bears unusual green flowers about 20 mm wide, which are almost translucent, and fade to orange. The sepals are flat and the petals narrow. The flowering period is from December to March. It is confined to high altitudes.

Calanthe sylvatica (=C. natalensis)

It is a rare privilege to find this orchid in the forest. It is about 400 mm high when in flower with broad, longitudinally pleated leaves and pretty lilac flowers. The flower is 40–50 mm wide and has spreading petals and sepals, a 2-lobed lip and a slender spur about 25 mm long. Flowering takes place from November to January. Recorded from a few localities on the central and southern mountains.

Ansellia gigantea var. *gigantea*

This *Ansellia* is one of the best-known orchids in the Lowveld and is frequently cultivated in gardens. It is an epiphyte with its densely massed roots firmly anchored on branches of trees. The long, slender pseudobulbs bear narrow, leathery leaves and striking, branched inflorescences. The fragrant yellow flowers, about 25 mm wide, are plain or have faint brown markings and the short lip has raised crests. The flowers open during August and September. This orchid is remarkably adaptable: it is often seen in hot, dry, exposed situations e.g. in a dead Leadwood tree in the Kruger National Park, but it is equally at home in shade, in an evergreen Waterberry in the Nelspruit district. Widely distributed over the Lowveld.

Ansellia gigantea var. *nilotica* Leopard Orchid, Luiperdorgidee

When not in bloom this epiphyte cannot be distinguished from the typical var. *gigantea*. The magnificent flowers are, however, unmistakable: they have bold, dark brown blotches and are slightly larger, up to 30 mm wide. Flowering takes place from September to November. Not quite as common as the typical variety, it is also distributed over the whole Lowveld, being slightly more abundant in the north.

Liparis bowkeri (=L. neglecta)

Calanthe sylvatica (=C. natalensis)

Ansellia gigantea var. *gigantea*

Ansellia gigantea var. *nilotica*

ORCHIDACEAE

Eulophia angolensis Vlei Orchid, Vlei-orgidee

This splendid orchid grows in profusion in some local vleis where it often flowers alongside *Dissotis canescens* (plate 138), providing a wonderful display of colour. When in flower it is up to 2 m high with narrow, shallowly pleated leaves and fragrant, clear yellow flowers. The narrow sepals are erect, about 20 mm long and the broad petals overlap forwards over the crested lip. Flowering takes place from December to February. Recorded from numerous localities at various altitudes from north to south.

Eulophia foliosa

A delightful orchid up to 400 mm high when in flower with narrow leaves which are slightly ribbed and a short, dense inflorescence with pretty, lime-green flowers. The petals and sepals are more or less equal, about 15 mm long and the contrasting lip is white with chocolate or purple at the tip. Flowering takes place from November to January. Recorded in open grassland on the central and southern escarpment and foothills.

Eulophia fridericii

This dainty little woodland orchid is 200–300 mm high with a few leaves on a short shoot separate from the flowering stem. The flowers have erect, brown sepals with undulate, yellow margins and there are red stripes along the veins of the yellow petals and also on the lip. Sepals and petals are all about 8 mm long. Flowering takes place from October to December. Found in humus, this rare orchid has been recorded from only a few scattered localities in the Lowveld.

Eulophia horsfallii Purple Vlei Orchid, Persvleiorgidee

This stunning orchid has a regal quality and is perhaps the finest *Eulophia* of all. It is robust and up to 2 m high when in flower, with leaves up to 1 m long and the superb flowers are up to 50 mm wide. The maroon sepals are narrow and the mauve petals are rounded, held over the large, purple lip which has an undulate margin and 3 parallel, snow-white crests. The flowering period is erratic, occurring at any time between September and June. It grows in vleis and riverine bush at varying altitudes in the central and southern districts.

Eulophia angolensis

Eulophia foliosa

Eulophia fridericii

Eulophia horsfallii

ORCHIDACEAE

Eulophia ovalis subsp. *bainesii*

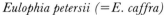

An orchid of rocky grassland areas, this *Eulophia* is up to 500 mm high, with leaves of varying lengths and a relatively short inflorescence. The narrow sepals are chocolate or greeny-brown and the oblong, cream petals partially obscure the cream lip which has bright yellow crests. Sepals and petals are about 25 mm long and flowering usually takes place in midsummer. Recorded from the southern mountains.

Eulophia petersii (=E. caffra)

Tall and handsome, this *Eulophia* grows up to 2 m high when in fllower with robust, exposed pseudobulbs, thick, rigid leaves and numerous fragrant flowers which are usually widely spaced. The narrow, purply-green sepals are about 25 mm long and the green petals have their tips rolled back tightly. The white lip has an undulate margin and mauve crests and the hooked, red spur is about 8 mm long. Flowering takes place from November to February. It forms clumps in rock crevices and shallow rock depressions, mainly at medium altitudes in the central and southern regions.

Eulophia speciosa

This sturdy, hardy orchid is 400–600 mm high, with thick, stiff leaves and well-spaced, brilliant yellow flowers which are 30–40 mm wide. The short light-green sepals are folded back, the petals flare out to the sides and the yellow-crested lip has a few maroon stripes. Flowering takes place from October to December. It grows in open woodland, generally in sandy soil and has been recorded from a few scattered localities in the central and southern regions.

Eulophia streptopetala

Tall, slim and elegant, this is one of the most striking Eulophias of the region. It is a hardy plant, up to 2 m high when in flower, with pleated leaves and captivating, well-spaced flowers which are up to 40 mm wide. The oval sepals are mottled with green-and-chocolate, and the round, bright yellow petals are carried horizontally, over the folded lip. Flowering takes place from September to December. Occurring at various altitudes in open, rocky woodland, it is widely distributed in the central and southern regions.

Eulophia ovalis subsp. *bainesii*

Eulophia petersii (=E. caffra)

Eulophia speciosa

Eulophia streptopetala

ORCHIDACEAE

Acampe praemorsa (=A. pachyglossa)

This rather rare epiphyte is inconspicuous for most of the year. It is a robust plant with sturdy roots and thick, strap-shaped leaves folded upwards along the length. The fragrant flowers, about 25 mm wide, are yellow with red or purple blotches and have a hard, waxy texture. The white lip is also marked and ages to pink. Flowers briefly, during January and February. Found on trees on stream banks, it has been recorded from only a few localities in the central and northern Lowveld.

Mystacidium capense

This is one of the most beautiful species within the small-flowered genus *Mystacidium*. It is an epiphyte with leathery, strap-shaped leaves and green roots streaked with white. There are 1–4 inflorescences with dainty, snow-white flowers which are about 20 mm wide. The sepals are longer than the petals and lip, and the spur is about 50 mm long. Flowering takes place from October to January. Recorded from a few localities in the central and southern districts.

Cyrtorchis arcuata

Of the two species of *Cyrtorchis* featured here, *C. arcuata* is easily distinguished by its large flowers. It is a robust epiphyte with strong roots which have orange growing tips and stiff, strap-shaped leaves. It bears 2–6 graceful, arched inflorescences, each with approximately 10 creamy-white flowers, up to 30 mm wide, which mature to orange. The slender spurs are about 30 mm long and flowering takes place from January to March. Relatively rare in this region, it has been recorded from only a few localities in the central and southern area, where it grows on trees in riverine forest.

Cyrtorchis praetermissa var. praetermissa

This species is, in general, very similar to *C. arcuata* but is less robust, with smaller dimensions. The fragrant ivory flowers are about 13 mm wide and the slender greenish spurs, which are almost transparent, are 20–30 mm long. Flowering takes place during November and December. This epiphyte forms little colonies in forested, hilly areas and on the banks of streams along the escarpment and foothills.

Acampe praemorsa (=A. pachyglossa)

Mystacidium capense

Cyrtorchis arcuata

Cyrtorchis praetermissa var. *praetermissa*

MORACEAE

The wild figs, which belong to this family, are deciduous to semi-deciduous trees which produce latex and have pale bark. They bear figs which are eaten by birds and animals and, occasionally, humans. The fig is a compound fruit with tiny flowers on the inside which are pollinated by small wasps and other insects which gain entry through the opening at the apex of the fig. In most cases fruiting takes place irregularly.

Ficus sycomorus Sycamore Fig, Gewone Trosvy

Probably the best-known wild fig in the Lowveld, this majestic tree can become 20 m high and the tall trunk often has spectacular buttresses. The rough-textured, oval to roundish leaves are about 100 mm long and the velvety, red figs, with paler flecks, are about 30 mm in diameter. They are borne in enormous, branched bunches from the trunk and on mature wood. Confined to the lower altitudes, it is common along the rivers, but does occasionally also occur in grassland where the rainfall is sufficient. There are some magnificent specimens at Pafuri in the Kruger National Park.

Ficus sur (=F. capensis) Broom Cluster Fig, Besemtrosvy

About 8 m high, this medium-sized tree has smooth, broad, oval leaves with undulate, irregularly dentate margins, up to 200 mm long. The smooth, fleshy figs, up to 30 mm in diameter, are red with paler streaks and hang in large bunches from mature wood. As shown in the illustration, figs are sometimes also borne on the roots, at or just below ground level. Found at various altitudes in open or rocky grassland and along watercourses, throughout the area, except in the arid regions.

Ficus ingens Red-leaved Rock Fig, Rooiblaarrotsvy

The most distinctive and striking feature of this small to medium-sized tree is its brilliant red or copper spring foliage. When seen in the early morning light the tree blazes with colour. The smooth, hard leaves are spear-shaped and up to 150 mm long. The smooth yellow figs, usually in pairs, are about 10 mm in diameter and are borne towards the tips of young branches. Occurs at various altitudes, generally in rocky places and has been extensively recorded throughout the entire region.

Ficus sycomorus

F. sycomorus

Ficus sur (= F. capensis)

Ficus ingens

MORACEA

Ficus sonderi Mountain Rock Fig, Bergrotsvy

This small to medium-sized tree grows up to 13 m high and has conspicuously shaggy young growth. The hard leaves are more or less oblong and about 120 mm long, with undulate margins. Large, red-brown stipules remain at the tips of young shoots for some time. This striking wild fig is found on rocky outcrops at various altitudes, in scattered localities throughout the entire region, with the exception of the arid areas.

Ficus abutilifolia (=F. soldanella) Large-leaved Rock Fig, Groot-blaarrotsvy

This small tree is invariably associated with boulders and rock faces and is distinguished by its large leaves and very white bark. It usually branches near the base, the exceptionally white roots spreading over, under and between boulders and into crevices, in search of soil and sustenance. The smooth, round leaves have undulate margins and are up to 200 mm in diameter. Single or paired, the slightly velvety, red figs, about 20 mm in diameter, are borne on new growth. Found mainly at low altitudes, this distinctive tree grows on rocky outcrops and inaccessible cliff faces throughout the Lowveld.

Ficus sansibarica (=F. brachylepis) Knobbly Fig, Angola Fig, Knoppiesvy, Angolawildevy.

This rather rare tree can be up to 20 m high and is sometimes a strangler: seed, distributed by birds or animals, may germinate in the fork of another tree and the vigorous roots of the wild fig, in search of soil, eventually completely encompass the trunk of the host tree. The Knobbly Fig has smooth, narrow oblong leaves up to 120 mm long. The large, smooth figs, purply-red with yellow flecks when ripe, are about 50 mm in diameter and are borne singly or in small clusters on mature wood; sometimes in great abundance, giving the tree a knobbly appearance. It grows in low-lying woodland and has been recorded from Pafuri, Sibasa, Tzaneen, Blyde River Canyon and Crocodile Gorge. Some fine planted specimens can be seen in Olifants Camp in the Kruger National Park.

Ficus sonderi

F. sonderi

Ficus abutilifolia (=F. soldanella)

Ficus sansibarica (=F. brachylepis)

PROTEACEAE

Proteus, a deity of classical mythology, possessed the power to change his form at will and this was probably why the name Proteaceae was chosen for this rich and diversified family of plants, of which only the genera *Faurea* and *Protea* are featured here, Faureas are small to medium evergreen trees with elongated inflorescences which, when in fruit, resemble large silky caterpillars and remain on the trees for some time.

Faurea galpinii Bush Beech, Forest Beechwood, Bosboekenhout

It is generally 4–5 m high, but reaches up to 10 m in forest and has narrow, tapering leaves up to 100 mm long, with undulate margins. The inflorescences, 80–100 mm long, are usually erect, with numerous small, white to creamy-mauve flowers which contrast beautifully with the glossy, dark-green leaves. Flowering is from December to March. A tree of forest and forest margins, it has been recorded from the central and southern escarpment.

Faurea saligna Transvaal Beechwood, Transvaalboekenhout

Well-known over a large part of the Transvaal, it is 6–12 m high, with shallowly fissured bark. The narrow, lanceolate to sickle-shaped leaves have undulate margins, are up to 120 mm long and turn red in winter. The slender, pendent inflorescences are up to 100 mm long, with small, fragrant, cream or pale-green flowers which open from August to February. The wood has an attractive reticulate grain and is sometimes used for furniture. Grows in open woodland and on rocky slopes along the escarpment and foothills.

Faurea speciosa Broad-leaved Beech, Breëblaarboekenhout

This small, rugged tree is distinguished by its large leaves and inflorescences, and deeply fissured bark. The shiny, undulate leaves are thick and leathery and up to 150 mm long. The robust inflorescences, erect or pendent, are up to 200 mm long with numerous ivory or dusty-pink flowers. Flowering is erratic, but mainly from February to September. Recorded from the central and southern escarpment and foothills, on open or lightly wooded, rocky slopes.

The Lowveld proteas are small evergreen trees or shrubs with slender leaves which often have red or yellow margins and midribs. The *Protea* inflorescence consists of numerous small flowers crowded in the centre, supported and surrounded by involucral bracts which are often showy and attractively coloured.

Protea caffra (=P. rhodantha, P. multibracteata) Common Sugarbush, Gewone Suikerbos

One of the commonest and most widespread proteas in South Africa. It is 3–7 m high and the flower heads, about 80 mm wide, are white and various shades of pink and red. Flowering takes place from October to March. This tree is common on the escarpment and foothills and grows on rocky slopes and ridges.

Faurea galpinii

Faurea saligna

Faurea speciosa

Protea caffra (=P. rhodantha, P. multibracteata)

PROTEACEAE

Protea comptonii Barberton Mountain Protea, Barbertonse Bergsuikerbos

This is one of the rarest and most spectacular proteas in the region. It is 4–5 m high and often has a crooked, gnarled trunk. The superb flower heads are up to 140 mm wide and the cream-and-white flowers, with faint red markings, are surrounded by creamy-yellow bracts. Flowering takes place from June to August. Until recently it was known only from a few steep slopes between Barberton and Havelock, near the summit of the pass, but has since also been collected in Swaziland.

Protea gaguedi African Protea, Afrikaanse Suikerbos

A shrub or small tree, it reaches up to 5 m in height and has a gnarled trunk. The relatively small flower heads are about 80 mm wide, with white or delicate pink flowers surrounded by creamy-green bracts. Flowering takes place from September to March. It grows on rocky slopes along the escarpment and foothills.

Protea laetans Blyde River Protea, Blyderivierprotea

Known only from the Blyde River Canyon, it was "discovered" as recently as 1970. It is a slender shrub or tree up to 5 m high with shiny silver bracts which give the unopened bud a distinctive appearance. The flower head is about 90 mm wide. The scarlet-and-tan flowers are surrounded by bracts which are scarlet on the inside. The flowering period is from March to September and specimens can be seen in the F. H. Odendaal Camp at Blyde River Canyon, as well as on the mountain slopes to the north-west of the camp.

Protea parvula

This attractive dwarf shrub is often hidden in grass or behind boulders and has procumbent stems up to 1 m long. The exquisite inflorescence, 60–80 mm wide, has flowers that are white or warm pink, surrounded by long, pink-and-cream bracts. The flowering period is from November to March. It is confined to the central and southern escarpment where it grows in open rocky grassland.

Protea comptonii

Protea gaguedi

Protea laetans

Protea parvula

PROTEACEAE

Protea roupelliae subsp. *roupelliae* Silver Protea, Silver Sugarbush, Silwersuikerbos

This tree is a well-known feature of grassy slopes and rocky outcrops along the escarpment, and is about 4 m high. The inflorescence is about 90 mm wide, with pink-and-white or cream-and-brown flowers and is characterised by the long spoon-shaped bracts which vary from cream to pink or red. The flowering period is from April to June and it has been recorded from the central and southern mountains.

Protea roupelliae subsp. *hamiltonii*

A dwarf, prostrate shrub up to 300 mm high with a spread of about 1 m. The inflorescence is very similar to that of subsp. *roupelliae*. Only the small size and growth habit of the plant distinguish it from the typical subspecies. This very rare *Protea* occurs in only a few colonies in a small area at Nelshoogte State Forest, near Barberton. The habitat is fragile, but the plants enjoy careful protection in the Dr. Hamilton Protea Reserve, especially proclaimed for this purpose. It flowers in summer, from December to March.

Protea rubropilosa Velvet Protea, Transvaal Mountain Sugarbush, Transvaalse Bergsuikerbos

From late winter into early spring the breath-taking, hazy-blue scenery at Blyde River Canyon is enhanced by the crimson inflorescences of one of the finest proteas in the region. It is a sturdy mountain shrub or small tree, normally 3–4 m high with stunning inflorescences about 110 mm wide. The massed red-and-white flowers are surrounded by crimson bracts which are velvety, deep red-brown on the outside. The name *rubropilosa* means "soft red hairs" and refers to the velvety texture which is so distinctive of this protea and imparts a unique appearance to the unopened bud. The flowering period is from August to November. Rather localised, this tree is known only from the central escarpment.

Protea roupelliae subsp. *roupelliae*

Protea roupelliae subsp. *hamiltonii*

Protea rubropilosa

P. rubropilosa

LORANTHACEAE

The plants featured here are parasites which grow on shrubs or trees, sometimes developing large, woody bases and branches 1–2 m long. The Afrikaans name Voëlent, which means "grafted on by birds" is most appropriate for this is exactly what happens: birds wipe the very sticky seeds off their bills and legs onto branches, where they soon become established. The slender, clustered flowers of the 4 species shown in the text open explosively at the merest touch, thereby dispersing the ripe pollen, after which the filaments usually curl up tightly. People throughly enjoy "popping" the flowers.

Erianthemum dregei (=Loranthus dregei) Mistletoe, Voëlent

The young leaves and twigs are velvet-brown, becoming smooth when mature. The very hairy flowers are about 50 mm long and are creamy-green and orange. The basal swelling of the corolla tube is inconspicuous and the long, slender lobes reflex after the flower opens. The flowering period is irregular, but occurs mainly from June to December. It grows in mixed woodland on a variety of hosts, e.g. *Acacia, Combretum, Maytenus, Strychnos* and *Trichilia*, and has been recorded from numerous localities throughout the Lowveld and escarpment.

Tapinanthus forbesii (=Loranthus oleifolius var. *forbesii)* Mistletoe, Voëlent

The showy flowers of this robust parasite are about 40 mm long. The smooth corolla tube is soft red with pale green markings and the oblong basal swelling is also green. The short lobes, charcoal-green inside, reflex after the flower opens. The flowering period is mainly from September to May. It has been recorded in mixed woodland from the south only, where it parasitises various species of *Acacia* and, particularly, *Sterculia murex*.

Tapinanthus kraussianus subsp. *transvaalensis (=Loranthus kraussianus* subsp. *transvaalensis)* Mistletoe, Voëlent

These colourful, conspicuous flowers are green and bright orange. The smooth corolla tube is about 40 mm long with a round basal swelling and the short orange lobes remain erect after the flower opens. The flowering period is mainly from December to March. It has been recorded in the south in low altitude, mixed woodland, on certain species of *Acacia* and *Combretum*.

Tapinanthus natalitius subsp. *zeyheri (=Loranthus zeyheri* var. *minor)* Mistletoe, Voëlent

One of the most beautiful plants in this genus, it has magnificent, nectar-laden flowers about 60 mm long. The smooth or slightly cobbled, white corolla tube, dull pink on the inside, has a round basal swelling and the short yellow lobes remain erect after the flower opens. Flowering usually takes place from October to February. Hosts include species of *Acacia* and *Combretum*. Recorded in mixed woodland from scattered localities in the central and southern mountains and foothills.

Erianthemum dregei (=Loranthus dregei)

Tapinanthus forbesii (=Loranthus oleifolius var. *forbesii)*

Tapinanthus kraussianus subsp. *transvaalensis*
   (=Loranthus kraussianus subsp. *transvaalensis)*

Tapinanthus natalitius subsp. *zeyheri*
   (=Loranthus zeyheri var. *minor)*

POLYGONACEAE
Rumex sagittatus Sorrel, Climbing Sorrel, Klimsuring, Ranksuring
This vigorous scrambler, related to the Coral Creeper found in gardens, has long, trailing stems and heart-shaped leaves. The attractive, dense inflorescence has massed tiny, pale green flowers up to 10 mm long which become russet-red and papery, remaining on the plant for some time. Flowering occurs from February to June. It grows on forest margins and stream banks, sometimes in rocky grassland, usually at medium to high altitudes, from north to south.

NYMPHAEACEAE
Nymphaea caerulea Water Lily, Blue Lotus, Waterlelie
This well-known aquatic plant, known as the Blue Lotus, must not be confused with the true Lotus Lily of the East. It has a submerged rhizome which roots in the mud floor of ponds or quiet streams and the floating leaf blade, almost circular, has a deep V-notch at the base. The beautiful flower, palest mauve to violet, has numerous petals which are about 50 mm long, and opens mainly from mid-summer to late autumn. It has been recorded from a few scattered localities at medium altitudes.

RANUNCULACEAE
Clematis brachiata Traveller's Joy, Old Man's Beard, Klimop,
   Lemoenbloeisels
A delightful climber which festoons trees, shrubs and even grassy banks with its abundant flowers, bringing joy to those who travel on the local roads during autumn. It has vigorous stems but no tendrils, climbing by means of strong, twining petioles. The delicate, fragrant flowers have no petals but there are 4 showy sepals and numerous radiating stamens, all cream or white. The massed fluffy fruits which follow the flowers, give the impression of an old man's beard. It grows in open woodland and on forest margins at various altitudes and is widely distributed over the entire region.

ROSACEAE

Leucosidea sericea Ouhout, Oudehout
Evocative of cold, crystal clear streams and misty mornings in the mountains, this rugged, aromatic tree is full of contrasts: the trunk is gnarled and crooked with rough, brittle bark while the grey-green pinnate leaves have a soft, silky texture. The dense inflorescence, 60–80 mm long, has small starry flowers which are creamy-green and open from about August to December. Concentrated on the escarpment in the Sabie-Graskop area.

Rumex sagittatus

Nymphaea caerulea

Clematis brachiata

Leucosidea sericea

CRASSULACEAE
Members of this family are often fleshy and succulent.

Kalanchoe rotundifolia
Erect or straggly and sometimes multi-stemmed, it is 300–400 mm high with rounded or oval leaves which vary in size. The somewhat flattened inflorescence is sparsely branched, with tiny orange to red flowers which open from March to August. The leaves and flowers are poisonous. It forms little colonies in light shade on rocky outcrops along the whole escarpment and foothills.

Kalanchoe thyrsiflora Meelplakkie
The Afrikaans name Meelplakkie is most appropriate for it does indeed look as though this whole plant has been liberally dusted with flour ("meel"). It is up to 600 mm high and the obovate leaves are flushed with red on the margins. The dense inflorescence has small tubular flowers about 15 mm long. The plant takes 3–4 years to mature before flowering, which normally takes place from February to June. It has been recorded from the central and southern escarpment and foothills, on open, rocky situations.

Crassula acinaciformis Giant Crassula, Reuseplakkie
Perhaps Cauliflower Crassula would be a good name for this tall, handsome perennial with its enormous inflorescence. It grows up to 2 m high and has a basal rosette of yellow-green leaves. The impressive head, 300–400 mm wide, is flat or slightly domed, with massed, tiny cream flowers which have a lovely wild-honey fragrance. The flowering period is from January to June. The plant takes 3–4 years to mature and flower, after which it dies. Found on moist slopes and in open woodland on the central and southern mountains and foothills.

Crassula alba var. *alba (= C. rubicunda)*
This attractive perennial reaches up to 500 mm high with narrow basal leaves. The flattened inflorescence, about 100–150 mm wide, consists of small flowers varying from pale pink to red and, rarely, white. The flowering period is from January to April. It grows in lightly shaded, rocky places on the central and southern mountains and foothills.

Kalanchoe rotundifolia

Kalanchoe thyrsiflora

Crassula acinaciformis

Crassula alba var. *alba (= C. rubicunda)*

CRASSULACEAE

Crassula globularioides subsp. argyrophylla

A gregarious little rock dweller up to 150 mm high, covered with very short, fine white hairs. The leaves are normally grey-green, but become rusty-red in dry, exposed situations. The almost globular inflorescence is 20–25 mm wide, with tiny white flowers which may open from April to September. It occurs in densely matted colonies on open rock faces on the central and southern mountains and foothills.

Crassula perfoliata subsp. heterotricha

This charming *Crassula* is about 300 mm high with woody stems and keeled, strap-shaped leaves. The inflorescence is slightly rounded and 60–80 mm wide and the fragrant little flowers are snow-white with bright red styles. Flowering takes place from April to June. It has a rather limited distribution, having been recorded only in the south, where it grows amongst granite boulders of medium altitudes.

Crassula sarcocaulis subsp. sarcocaulis (= C. parvisepala)

This unusual "miniature tree" looks like a natural Bonsai nestled amongst the weathered, lichen-covered rocks on the escarpment. It is generally 300–400 mm high with tiny narrow leaves near the tips of the branches. The inflorescence, about 20 mm wide, is a cluster of small creamy-yellow flowers with protruding black anthers and an unpleasant odour. Flowering occurs from October to March. Recorded from the central and southern mountains.

Crassula vaginata

Whether it is growing on its own or as part of a colony, this striking *Crassula* always catches the eye. It grows up to 400 mm high and the stem is usually unbranched. The inflorescence, up to 100 mm wide, is more or less flat-topped with numerous tiny flowers varying from cream to blazing, iridescent yellow. Flowering takes place from November to March. Generally found in open grassland on the central and southern mountains.

Crassula globularioides subsp. *argyrophylla*

Crassula perfoliata subsp. *heterotricha*

Crassula sarcocaulis subsp. *sarcocaulis* (= *C. parvisepala*)

Crassula vaginata

FABACEAE (=Leguminosae)

The trees, shrubs and herbacious plants of the well-known legume family usually bear 2-valved pods that split open.

FABACEAE Sub-family MIMOSOIDEAE

Albizia versicolor Large-leaved False Thorn, False Kiaat, Grootblaarvalsdoring, Sandkiaat

In general appearance resembling the true Kiaat, *Pterocarpus angolensis*, this striking tree is up to 15 m high and, like all albizias, has no thorns. The growing tips are rusty coloured and velvety and the pinnate leaves, up to 200 mm long, have rounded leaflets. The inflorescence is a powder-puff of small flowers with no petals but very showy stamens which are usually cream and about 30 mm long. Flowering takes place from October to November, simultaneously with the appearance of the new, coppery foliage. The flat pods, red-brown to deep crimson, are about 180 mm long and remain on the tree for a year or longer. The pods are poisonous, especially the seeds, and can be fatal to domestic stock. Mainly found in the Lowveld, but occasionally also occurring at medium altitudes, it grows in sandy or well-drained granitic soils, in open woodland and along the banks of streams.

Acacias are deciduous trees with bipinnate leaves and compound inflorescences, either elongated spikes or spherical heads. They have thorns which are usually paired and of varying lengths.

Acacia ataxacantha Flame Thorn, Vlamdoring

The common name refers to the beautiful red pods of this vigorous tree-scrambler that can form a smothering blanket over the tree canopy. It has small but strong, hooked thorns scattered along the stems and branches. The leaves are up to 150 mm long, with very fine leaflets and the inflorescences are fragrant cream spikes which open from November to April. The narrow, flattish pods, about 80 mm long, are usually of a remarkable red hue and are borne in clusters from March to June. Although this plant can spread and proliferate quite alarmingly, it is a splendid sight in flower or fruit. Found at various altitudes in densely wooded places in scattered localities over the entire region.

Albizia versicolor

Acacia ataxacantha

A. versicolor

A. ataxacantha

FABACEAE Sub-family MIMOSOIDEAE

Acacia gerrardii Red Thorn, Rooidoring

This *Acacia*, about 8 or 9 m high, has a rough fissured bark, revealing a red inner bark. The paired spines are usually straight and the leaves about 40 mm long. A beautiful sight in full bloom, it has spherical, cream heads about 10 mm in diameter. Flowering period is from August to March. It has slender "new-moon" pods about 100 mm long and grows in low to medium altitude woodland. Recorded from scattered localities from north to south. There are a few fine specimens in the Lowveld Botanic Garden at Nelspruit.

Acacia karroo Sweet Thorn, Soetdoring

One of the best-known and most widespread acacias of South Africa. It grows up to 8 m high with a fairly dense, rounded crown and has paired, white spines, and leaves up to 120 mm long. Fragrant, bright yellow, spherical heads, about 15 mm in diameter, are usually borne from October to January. The sickle-shaped pods are about 120 mm long. This *Acacia*, which grows in low to medium altitude open or scrubby woodland is widely distributed in the Lowveld and foothills.

Acacia nigrescens Knob Thorn, Knoppiesdoring

This well-known Lowveld tree derives its vernacular name from the thorn-tipped knobs on the bark, which are sometimes evident only on young wood. It is 10–20 m high with a relatively narrow crown and dark, hooked thorns, in pairs. The distinctive leaves have only 2–6 pairs of roundish, blue-green leaflets. Pink buds open into fragrant cream spikes about 100 mm long and the tree is a delight of delicate colour during August and September. The narrow pods, about 120 mm long, are black when mature as implied by the name *nigrescens*, meaning "becoming black". Extensively recorded in the dry woodland of the Lowveld.

Acacia nilotica subsp. *kraussiana* Scented Thorn, Lekkerruikpeul

Distinctively flat-topped, this relatively small *Acacia* grows up to 6 m high. The slender whitish thorns are paired and the leaves are 40–50 mm long. The fragrant spherical flower heads are bright yellow and about 10 mm in diameter, opening from November to January. The narrow pods, 80–150 mm long and constricted around the seeds, have a strong fruity aroma and are eaten readily by game and domestic stock. Grows in various types of scrub and woodland over the entire Lowveld.

Acacia gerrardii

Acacia karroo

Acacia nigrescens

Acacia nilotica subsp. *kraussiana*

FABACEAE Sub-family MIMOSOIDEAE

Acacia sieberana var. *woodii* Paperbark Thorn, Papierbasdoring

Near Barberton, on the road to Nelspruit, one drives through an impressive avenue of stately Paperbark Thorn trees which are characterised by the corky, yellow-grey bark which peels off in papery flakes. The paired spines are white or grey and the leaves up to 150 mm long. The fragrant, creamy flower heads are spherical, up to 15 mm in diameter and open from October to December. The thick woody pods are about 120 mm long. Grows in open woodland which is often park-like, in the Lowveld and foothills, mainly in the central and southern regions.

Acacia tortilis subsp. *heteracantha* Umbrella Thorn, Haak-en-steek

With its characteristic flat umbrella crown, this *Acacia* is a conspicuous feature of open parkland in the Lowveld. It is 5–10 m high with paired spines that may be straight or hooked or one of each in a pair: hence the appropriate Afrikaans name Haak-en-steek (hook-and-prick). The small, sparse leaves are only about 30 mm long and the tiny, scented, creamy-white heads are spherical and about 8 mm in diameter. The flowering period is from November to January. The narrow, yellow-brown pods are distinctively coiled and contorted. Occurs throughout the Lowveld, and there are some outstanding specimens along the Timbavati Road in the Kruger National Park.

Acacia xanthophloea Fever Tree, Koorsboom

Because this tree grows in marshy areas and along the banks of rivers, which are the breeding places of mosquitoes, it has always been associated with malaria, hence the common name. It can be up to 15 m high and a distinctive powdery, yellow-green layer covers the green bark. The paired spines are straight and white and the leaves have tiny leaflets, giving the crown an open, airy appearance. The bright yellow, spherical flower heads are about 10 mm in diameter and open from September to November. The narrow pods are about 100 mm long. The Fever Tree is common in the low-lying eastern regions.

Dichrostachys cinerea subsp. *nyassana* Large-leaved Sickle Bush, Chinese Lantern Tree, Grootblaarsekelbos

Acacia-like in general appearance, this shrub or small tree is 2–4 m high and has thick hard spines which occur singly. The charming pendent inflorescences, pink and yellow, are like little Chinese Lanterns, and they festoon the crown from October to January. The flat pods, which change from pale green to chocolate as they ripen, are borne in attractive tangled clusters and are readily eaten by game and domestic stock. The medicinal uses of various parts of the tree are legion, while the stem is highly prized as firewood and for making handles for small tools. Widely distributed in low to medium altitudes, open or lightly wooded grassland.

Acacia sieberana var. *woodii*

Acacia tortilis subsp. *heteracantha*

Acacia xanthophloea

Dichrostachys cinerea subsp. *nyassana*

FABACEAE Sub-family CAESALPINIOIDEAE

Schotia brachypetala Weeping Boer-bean, Tree Fuchsia, Weeping Schotia, Huilboerboom.

This magnificent tree weeps, but its tears are sweet: it has an over-abundance of nectar which drips out of the flowers. Sometimes found on termite mounds, it can be up to 12 m high with a dense crown and glossy, dark green pinnate leaves. The crimson flowers, clustered on mature wood, have showy sepals about 8 mm long and they open during September and October, attracting sunbirds from sunrise to sunset. Petals are minute or absent, as suggested by the name "brachypetala", meaning "short petals". The seeds are eaten by birds and roasted for human consumption. It is a fast-growing, rewarding garden tree and is widely distributed in the Lowveld, where it grows on stream banks and in open woodland.

Peltophorum africanum African Wattle, Weeping Wattle, Huilboom

Another weeping tree, but its tears are in fact excretions from a little spittle bug producing large quantities of moisture which drip to the ground. The tree is 6–10 m high with bipinnate leaves and antler-shaped stipules which fall early and can thus usually be seen only on young growth. The showy inflorescence is a dense mass of yellow flowers with crinkly petals and flowering takes place from September to February. The flat oval pod tapers at both ends and has a compressed margin. Widely recorded in wooded or rocky grassland at low to medium altitudes.

Tylosema fassoglense (=Bauhinia fassoglensis)

A vigorous scrambler with bi-lobed leaves which sometimes have rusty coloured hairs on the lower surface, have a notch at the apex, and are up to 150 mm wide. The clear lemon flowers have 5 crinkly, paddle-shaped petals, 4 of them about 30 mm long and the 5th very much smaller. Flowering takes place mainly from October to January and the hard woody pods contain 2–3 seeds. Found on rocky or wooded slopes at various altitiudes, in scattered localities from north to south.

Bauhinia galpinii Pride-of-De Kaap, Vlam-van-die-Vlakte

This vigorous, well-known Lowveld plant, with its glorious, vivid flowers, is successfully grown in gardens, but in the Lowveld it has to be kept under control lest it swamp everything in sight! The blue-green, 2-lobed leaves, notched at the apex, are about 60 mm in diameter. The flowers are deep salmon to orange, with 5 crinkled, paddle-shaped petals up to 40 mm long, and appear from November to March. The hard woody pods contain a few flat seeds. Found at low to medium altitudes, it is common in wooded places and riverine thickets.

Schotia brachypetala

Peltophorum africanum

Tylosema fassoglense (=Bauhinia fassoglensis)

Bauhinia galpinii

FABACEAE Sub-family CAESALPINIOIDEAE

Cassia abbreviata subsp. *beareana* Sjambok Pod, Long Tail Cassia, Sambokpeul, Kersboom

Conspicuous when in flower or fruit, this arresting tree is a distinctive feature of the hot, dry Lowveld. It grows up to 5 m high with drooping pinnate leaves and bright yellow flowers, of which the stamens and style are gracefully arched upwards. Flowering takes place during September and October. The narrow, cylindrical pods become dark brown and up to 600 mm long, remaining on the tree for many months and splitting open with a twist. Recorded from north to south in open woodland at low altitudes. The seed germinates easily and it is a good subject for frost-free gardens.

Cassia petersiana Monkey Pod, Apiespeul

A showy, autumn-flowering shrub or small tree, it is normally 2–3 m high with pinnate leaves and characteristic stipules which are round and tailed. The dark yellow flowers have arched stamens and style, and open from January to May. The slender pods, constricted between the seeds, are up to 200 mm long. It is relatively common in low to medium atlitude woodland and riverine bush and is an excellent garden shrub.

Pterolobium stellatum

This attractive plant is conspicuous when in flower or in fruit. The generic name Pterolobium is derived from the Greek words meaning "wing" and "fruit", descriptive of the pods. So many of the scientific plant names are descriptive of a particular feature of the specific plant, that is worthwhile to make an attempt to learn these names and use them. *Pterolobium* is a vigorous scrambler, and is well-armed with vicious prickles. The bipinnate leaves are about 70 mm long, with prickles along the lower surface of the rachis. Flowering spikes are generally erect and about 100 mm long with numerous tiny, fragrant flowers which are soft creamy-yellow, opening from March to June and occasionally from December to February. The bright crimson pod is small and oval, with one thin, membranous wing. Found at low to medium altitudes in thick bush on rocky hillsides and road verges, this prickly but beautiful plant has been recorded from scattered localities from north to south.

Cassia abbreviata subsp. *beareana*

Cassia petersiana

Pterolobium stellatum

P. stellatum

FABACEAE Sub-family PAPILIONOIDEAE

Plants in this sub-family have flowers which are structurally similar to those of the sweetpea of horticulture.

Bolusanthus speciosus Tree Wistaria, Vanwykshout

This attractive tree, with its wistaria-like flowers, is an outstanding garden tree and there is an impressive avenue at the entrance to the Botanical Research Institute in Pretoria. It grows up to 6 m high, with a relatively narrow crown and graceful, drooping foliage. The pendent inflorescence is a loose spray of beautiful mauve to purple flowers which open during August and September. The flowering period of individual trees is brief but spectacular. Widely distributed over the whole Lowveld, in dry, open woodland.

Pearsonia aristata

A much-branched shrublet sparsely covered with hairs, growing up to 500 mm high. The leaves, as in all pearsonias, are trifoliate and the dark green leaflets each taper to a sharp, hard point. The bright yellow little flowers have bell-shaped calyxes and open from October to December. Grows in open, rocky grassland on the central and southern mountains.

Pearsonia cajanifolia

An attractive, bushy shrub up to 600 mm high with stems and leaves covered with fine, golden velvety hairs. The leaflets are up to 100 mm long, each ending in a little point. The inflorescence is round and compact, with small yellow flowers which open from October to December. It occurs in colonies in grassland and on rocky slopes and has been recorded from only a few localities on the central and southern mountains and foothills.

Pearsonia sessilifolia subsp. *filifolia*

Exquisite when in bloom, this bushy shrublet is 300–500 mm high. The very narrow leaflets are 15–30 mm long and there is a tuft of silky hairs at the base of the petiole. The gay, sunny little flowers appear during September and October. It grows on open or lightly wooded, rocky grassland and is not very common, having been recorded from only a few localities in the south, at low to medium altitudes.

Bolusanthus speciosus

Pearsonia aristata

Pearsonia cajanifolia

Pearsonia sessilifolia subsp. *filifolia*

FABACEAE Sub-family PAPILIONOIDEAE

Indigofera hilaris

This beautiful, bushy shrublet brightens up bare or burnt veld in spring and early summer. It is up to 400 mm high and has pinnate leaves with pale green, narrow leaflets. The small, clear pink flowers are borne in profusion from August to December. Grows in open, rocky grassland on the central and southern mountains and foothills.

◆ *Sesbania punicea*
PROCLAIMED WEED

This shrub or small tree, generally 1–2 m high, has drooping, bipinnate leaves and pretty, dark orange flowers borne in short, dense sprays during spring and early summer. The oblong, 4-winged pod is about 70 mm long. The leaves, flowers and seeds of this plant are lethally poisonous to certain animals and birds. Introduced from South America, its country of origin, it has escaped into the wild where it has proliferated alarmingly and now threatens to oust the indigenous vegetation. It is particularly rife and conspicuous along the rivers in this area.

Dalbergia armata Thorny Rope, Hluhluwe Creeper, Doringtou, Bobbejaantou

This is sometimes a shrub or small tree, but more often a rampant woody climber. Young branches twine around supporting vegetation, enabling the stems to climb up into the canopy, at times smothering it completely. Stems and branches are armed with hard, strong spines up to 150 mm long and the pinnate leaves have very small leaflets. Great masses of tiny, fragrant, creamy-white flowers are borne in abundance from October to December. Found at varying altitudes in wooded ravines, riverine bush and evergreen forest, from north to south.

Abrus precatorius subsp. *africanus* Lucky Bean Creeper

This climber is much more conspicuous and attractive in fruit than in flower. It has long, twining stems, pinnate leaves and short sprays with a few small mauve flowers. The clustered pods are very striking, each somewhat triangular and about 30 mm long, splitting open to display the shiny red-and-black "lucky bean" seeds. These conspicuous fruits decorate the bush from June to October. The seeds are extremely poisonous, containing a toxin, *abrin*, which is released if the hard seed-covering is broken, as for example, when chewed. All parts of the plant are used in tribal medicine, in the treatment of a variety of ailments. It grows in dry woodland at low to medium altitudes.

Indigofera hilaris

Sesbania punicea

Dalbergia armata

Abrus precatorius subsp. *africanus*

FABACEAE Sub-family PAPILIONOIDEAE

Erythrina latissima Broad-leaved Coral Tree, Breëblaarkoraalboom

This gnarled, rugged tree, with its dark, rough bark and magnificent crimson flowers is a study of contrasts in colour and texture making a bold statement in the winter landscape. It is 5–7 m high and has sharp, hooked prickles. All young growth is densely woolly, becoming smooth with age. The trifoliate leaves have large, leathery, almost circular leaflets about 200 mm in diameter. The superb inflorescence, the largest of the local erythrinas, is up to 150 mm in diameter, the corolla colour varying from scarlet to deep crimson. Flowering takes place from July to September. The large, thick-walled, woody pod is constricted around the big, black-and-red "lucky bean" seeds which are exposed when it splits open. This tree is a dramatic garden subject but unfortunately the soft, brittle wood is frequently borer-infested. Found on rocky mountain slopes and in open woodland, at medium to high altitudes in the central and southern regions.

Erythrina lysistemon Common Coral Tree, Gewone Koraalboom

One of the best-known trees, it brightens the winter landscape, to the delight of every camera-toting tourist who cannot resist the contrast of scarlet flowers against a hazy blue mountain backdrop. It is generally 6–8 m high, with pale yellow-grey bark and sharp, hooked prickles on the trunk and branches. The trifoliate leaves have soft leaflets, much smaller than those of the previous species, with tapering tips. The inflorescence is a showy head of brilliant scarlet flowers appearing from June to September. The black-brown pods are more slender and less woody than those of *E. latissima* and the seeds very much smaller. This is an outstanding and popular garden subject but may also have to be treated for borers. It has been utilised for a variety of purposes in tribal medicine. It is widely distributed in the Lowveld and on the foothills and grows in open or scrubby woodland.

Erythrina latissima

E. latissima

Erythrina lysistemon

E. lysistemon

FABACEAE Sub-family PAPILIONOIDEAE

Pterocarpus angolensis Kiaat, Transvaal Teak

The stately Kiaat is a tree for all seasons: in spring it is adorned with bright yellow flowers; in summer it has a graceful green appearance with its drooping foliage and young fruits; in autumn the leaves are golden-yellow and the fruits brown; and perhaps it is at its best in winter when, leafless, it displays the intricacy of its curved, contorted branches, still carrying the dry, brown fruits. It is a shapely tree up to 18 m high with characteristically fissured bark and, when cut, it exudes a sticky red sap. The pinnate leaves are up to 250 mm long and the fragrant flowers have crinkly petals. Flowering takes place from August to October, just before the new leaves appear. The distinctive circular fruit, up to 140 mm in diameter, has a broad undulating wing around a bristly seed case in the centre (it has been described as a "porcupine in a life-belt!"). The Kiaat is important in tribal culture: the sap is used as a dye and various parts of the tree are utilised in medicine and witchcraft. The beautiful wood is extremely popular in the manufacture of furniture and both utilitarian and ornamental articles. It is widely distributed in the Lowveld and on the foothills, in open parkland or mixed woodland.

Pterocarpus rotundifolius Round-leaved Kiaat, Dopperkiaat

Exquisite in full bloom and abuzz with bees all day long, this is one of the finest flowering trees of the region. It is up to 15 m high and the pinnate leaves, about 150 mm long, have 5–9 glossy, round leaflets. *Rotundifolius* means "round-leaved". The fragrant, crinkly, yellow flowers are borne in abundant profusion; a very brief flowering period occurring between October to January. Flowering usually coincides with the first good rains of the season. The roundish fruit is inconspicuous and tends to "disappear" into the foliage: it has a flattish wing and does not have the bristly centre of *P. angolensis*. Generally found in low to medium altitude open woodland, it is widely distributed from north to south.

Lonchocarpus capassa Apple-leaf, Rain Tree, Appelblaar

The common name implies a similarity to the apple tree but they are not related, the apple having simple leaves, whereas those of *Lonchocarpus* are compound. It is a medium-sized tree which can be up to 18 m high and the greygreen pinnate leaves have 3–5 leaflets, of which the terminal is by far the largest. Compact clusters of small flowers, borne briefly from September to November, transform this somewhat drab tree into a soft, fragrant cloud of blue-mauve mist. This is a true Lowveld tree of open woodland and stream banks. There are some large, impressive specimens in the Letaba Camp, at Pafuri and along the Timbavati Road in the Kruger National Park.

Pterocarpus angolensis

P. angolensis

Pterocarpus rotundifolius

Lonchocarpus capassa

FABACEAE Sub-family PAPILIONOIDEAE

Eriosema psoraleoides

Conspicuous in late summer, this bushy but single-stemmed shrub can be 1,5 m high. All the green parts are velvety and the trifoliate leaves have narrow leaflets about 100 mm long. The dense inflorescence consists of sunny-yellow flowers which open from December to March. The roundish pods are very shaggy, and approximately 15 mm long. Generally found in grassland at various altitudes in scattered localities in the central and southern districts.

Canavalia virosa

This handsome climber has horticultural potential and has been successfully cultivated in private gardens and the Lowveld Botanic Garden in Nelspruit. It is velvety, with twining stems and trifoliate leaves. The erect inflorescences have attractive pink to mauve flowers which open from February to April, and the pods are large velvety beans with 2 thick hard ridges. Found on forest margins at low altitudes. It is rather localised, having been recorded from only a few localities in the north and in the south.

Mucuna coriacea subsp. *irritans* Hellfire Bean, Brandboon, Jeukpeul

All its vernacular names adequately describe the extremely unpleasant reaction of skin contact to the pods of this plant. They are covered with fiercely irritant, minutely barbed hairs, therefore reducing its horticultural potential, for its flowers are superb. This vigorous scrambler has tough, twining stems and trifoliate leaves with blue-green leaflets. The compact inflorescences are clusters of magnificent burgundy flowers which open from March to April. They are followed by the beautiful but dangerous velvety pods which are golden-brown and 60–80 mm long. Extensively recorded from north to south, at low to medium altitudes. It grows in scrub or grassland and often on road verges and disturbed soil.

Eriosema psoraleoides

Canavalia virosa

Mucuna coriacea subsp. *irritans*

M. coriacea subsp. *irritans*

GERANIACEAE
Pelargonium lateripes Transvaal Ivy-leaved Pelargonium, Wildemalva

This scrambling plant, with trailing zig-zag stems, has great potential as a hardy ground cover in gardens. The succulent leaves, with 5–7 shallow lobes and faint red margins, are about 50 mm wide. The charming pale pink flowers have maroon markings and are borne in clusters of up to 10. They have 5 petals, each about 15 mm long and flowering takes place from August to January. Recorded from the banks of streams on the central escarpment in the Bourke's Luck area.

Pelargonium luridum Wild Pelargonium, Wildemalva

This beautiful *Pelargonium* is covered with soft hairs and is up to 60 mm high. The leaves, which form a basal rosette, vary greatly in shape and size. The inflorescence is a lax cluster, 100–130 mm wide, of cream to dusky pink flowers, opening from September to March. Recorded in damp grassland at medium to high altitudes, from north to south. Sometimes found on road verges where it benefits from run-off moisture.

OXALIDACEAE
Oxalis obliquifolia Oxalis, Sorrel, Suring

An enchanting little perennial about 100 mm high with small round bulbs and trifoliate leaves on slender petioles. The flowers are approximately 15 mm wide, with 5 petals which vary from snow-white to shades of pink, with yellow in the throat. Flowering takes place from December to March. It occurs in small colonies in grassland or recently disturbed soil at various altitudes in the central and southern areas.

RUTACEAE
Calodendrum capense Cape Chestnut, Wildekastaiing

This exceptional tree is conspicuous in densely wooded ravines, where its superb pink flowers stand out in the dark green canopy. It is one of the finest flowering trees in this region and is a most rewarding garden subject. It is up to 18 m high, with very dark green leaves which have transparent gland dots scattered over the blades — these can be seen when the leaves are held up against the light. The showy inflorescence consists of pale pink flowers, each up to 60 mm wide, with slender petals and stamens dotted with maroon. Flowering takes place from October to December. The woody brown fruit is a knobbly, 5-lobed capsule about 35 mm in diameter, which contains hard, black seeds. Recorded from scattered localities along the mountains and foothills.

Pelargonium lateripes

Pelargonium luridum

Oxalis obliquifolia

Calodendrum capense

BURSERACEAE

This is commonly known as the myrrh family because the fragrant resin of that name is obtained from one of the commiphoras of Arabia. Some of the local species also contain resin but are of no commercial significance. The local commiphoras are usually small trees, generally growing in dry bushveld and are easily identified by their distinctive bark. The small, inconspicuous male and female flowers are borne on separate trees during summer. The asymmetric, roundish fruit, 10–15 mm long, contains a stone which is partially covered by a 4-clawed fleshy cap which is yellow to red. The Afrikaans name kanniedood means "cannot die" and refers to the remarkable hardiness of the genus. If for example a tree was chopped down and the pieces left in the veld, each portion would probably take root and grow.

Commiphora harveyi Bronze Commiphora, Red-stem Corkwood, Rooistamkanniedood

Unlike the other commiphoras featured in the text this tree prefers a relatively moist environment. Its smooth green inner bark is covered by bronze and purplish flakes which peel off. The pinnate leaves are about 150 mm long with 3–5 glossy leaflets with coarsely serrated margins. They turn bright yellow in autumn. Occurs in open woodland, on rocky slopes and on river banks at various altitudes in the central and southern regions.

Commiphora marlothii Paperbark Commiphora, Paperbark Corkwood, Papierbaskanniedood

Large papery strips of outer bark flake off this tree, revealing the smooth, dark green inner bark. The hairy, pinnate leaves are up to 250 mm long with about 7 leaflets. Generally associated with rocky places of low to medium altitudes and has been recorded in the north, from the Pafuri area.

Commiphora merkeri Zebra Tree, Zebra-bark Corkwood, Sebrabaskanniedood

Appropriately named, this arresting, zebra-striped tree has white or palest grey bark liberally embellished with transverse, warty, black markings. The leaves are generally simple, occasionally trifoliate and are up to 50 mm long, with finely serrated margins. Recorded from the Pafuri area where it grows in low altitude, dry bushveld.

Commiphora tenuipetiolata Blue Commiphora, White-stem Corkwood, Bloukaniedood, Witstamkanniedood

This blue and white tree is a stunning sight, particularly in winter, when it has lost its foliage. The satiny, powder-blue to blue-green inner bark is revealed when large papery strips of the white outer bark peel off. The leaves, about 70 mm long, have 3–9 leaflets. Grows on rocky slopes in the low-lying dry bushveld around Punda Maria and Pafuri.

Commiphora harveyi

Commiphora marlothii

Commiphora merkeri

Commiphora tenuipetiolata

MELIACEAE

Turraea obtusifolia Small Honeysuckle Bush

A delightful, bushy little shrub about 1 m high with slender leaves which vary in shape and size but are generally about 30 mm long. The pretty, snow-white flowers are about 40 mm wide with 5 slender, flaring petals. The stamens are fused into a tube from which the style protrudes. Flowering takes place from December to February. The attractive 5-valved fruit looks like a miniature scarlet pumpkin. Although it is considered by some to be very poisonous, causing severe gastric irritation, it is nevertheless used medicinally, in the treatment of stomach and intestinal disorders. Found in rocky places at low to medium altitudes.

Trichilia emetica Mkuhlu, Natal Mahogany, Rooiessenhout

A magnificent evergreen tree up to 20 m high with a large spreading crown which throws a cool, dense shade. The pinnate leaves, up to 400 mm long, have glossy leaflets and the creamy-green flowers are borne in dense inflorescences from August to October. The fruit is a dull green, 3-lobed capsule, 30 mm in diameter and contains large black seeds partially covered by a dark red, waxy cap. A decoction of the bark of this tree is administered as an emetic. Common in low to medium altitude riverine bush and mixed woodland.

♦ *Melia azedarach* Syringa, Persian Lilac, Sering
INTRODUCED

This prolific intruder grows up to 10 m high and has soft bipinnate leaves and tiny mauve flowers borne in branched sprays from August to December. The bitter and poisonous, biscuit-coloured berries contain numerous seeds which germinate readily. Thickets develop rapidly around mature trees. Native to the Himalayas, it has escaped from cultivation and become naturalised in the Lowveld where it is a threat to the natural vegetation, especially along watercourses. Recorded from the central and southern Lowveld. Infestations are particularly serious along the Crocodile and Elands Rivers.

Turraea obtusifolia

T. obtusifolia

Trichilia emetica

Melia azedarach

MALPIGHIACEAE

Sphedamnocarpus pruriens var. *pruriens*

During late summer and early autumn this slender climber provides bright splashes of colour in the bush. It has lanceolate leaves up to 50 mm long and clustered yellow flowers with crinkly, paddle-shaped petals. Flowering takes place from December to March. The russet fruits are divided into 3 sections, each with a wing about 10 mm long. Found at various altitudes in scrub and woodland in the central and southern areas.

POLYGALACEAE

At first glance the polygalas appear to belong to the sweetpea family, but they are distinguished by a tufted, fluffy crest on the lower, keel-shaped petal. The 2 largest of the 5 sepals are petal-like and are called wings.

Polygala albida

This subtly hued, erect little perennial grows up to 300 mm high and has soft narrow leaves up to 70 mm long. The delicate, densely crowded flowers are pale green and white and a brief flowering period occurs, between January and April. Found at various altitudes in open or wooded grassland from a few localities in the central and southern regions.

Polygala hottentotta

This slender shrub is up to 1 m high with linear leaves 10–50 mm long. The enchanting little flowers are fairly close-set but only a few open at a time. The wings are pale green with dark green veins and the 2 top petals are mauve and about 4 mm long. The keel is white and purple with a feathery mauve crest. The flowering period is from September to March. Grows in open grassland or on forest fringes at medium to high altitudes in the central and southern regions.

Polygala virgata var. *decora*

This is one of the most beautiful local polygalas. It is an erect shrub up to 2 m high with narrow leaves about 40 mm long. The striking inflorescence has numerous magenta or purple flowers, the wings of which have slightly darker stripes. The flowering period is indifinite and sporadic, occurring throughout the year. Widely distributed at medium to high altitudes in scrubby grassland and on forest fringes.

Sphedamnocarpus pruriens var. *pruriens*

Polygala albida

Polygala hottentotta

Polygala virgata var. *decora*

EUPHORBIACEAE

Securinega virosa Snow Berry, Witbessie

This bushy shrub is quite stunning when in fruit. It is 1–2 m high with thin, soft leaves which are obovate to broad oval in shape and about 20 mm long. The inconspicuous, creamy-green flowers are 1–2 mm in diameter, male and female appearing on separate plants. Flowering takes place from October to January. The fleshy snow-white berries are 4–5 mm in diameter and are eaten by birds. Grows in rocky, bushy places at low to medium altitudes.

Acalypha peduncularis

Because the male and female plants bear differing flowers, they are frequently thought to be separate species. The plant has prostrate stems up to 300 mm long and shiny leaves up to 60 mm long with serrated margins. The erect male inflorescence has tiny red buds opening to white, presenting a charming picture, and the female inflorescence (not shown) is red and fluffy. Flowering takes place from September to February. Recorded from scattered localities in medium to high altitude grassland in the central and southern districts.

Clutia monticola

A bushy, leafy shrub up to 600 mm high with soft smooth leaves which are oval to narrow-obovate and up to 50 mm long. Young leaves are conspicuously yellow-green. The tiny flowers are pale green and normally open from August to November, followed by small, round, 3-valved fruits. Widespread in open grassland at medium to high altitudes.

Euphorbia cooperi Transvaal Candelabra Tree, Transvaalse Kandelaarnaboom

This striking, leafless tree grows about 5 m high and has a candelabra-shaped crown. The 5-angled branches have heart-shaped segments on the ridges of which short thorns and clusters of fleshy yellow flowers are borne. Flowering takes place from June to August, followed by triangular red fruits. This tree produces a latex which is a highly irritant substance and causes severe pain on eye-contact, resulting in temporary or permanent blindness, and even the vapour from the latex can cause a similar reaction. The latex is used as a fish poison. Grows on rocky outcrops and has been recorded from scattered localities, mainly at low to medium altitudes. It may perhaps be more wide-spread than is indicated by herbarium specimens which are both difficult and dangerous to make!

Securinega virosa

Acalypha peduncularis

Clutia monticola

Euphorbia cooperi

GREYIACEAE

Greyia radlkoferi Transvaal Bottlebrush, Transvaalse Baakhout

As rugged as its rocky, mountain environs, it is often gnarled and crooked, with very rough bark. It is 3–5 m high with shallowly lobed leaves which are nearly circular and up to 100 mm wide. They are felt-textured and white below and have coarsely toothed margins. The beautiful bottlebrush inflorescence consists of brilliant scarlet, bell-shaped flowers which are conspicuous amongst the lichened, weathered rocks. Flowering takes place from July to November. Recorded along the central and southern escarpment, mostly on the margins of forested ravines.

BALSAMINACEAE

Impatiens sylvicola Impatiens

This soft forest perennial is related to the Impatiens or Busy Lizzy, so popular in gardens. It grows up to 400 mm high with pale green, fleshy stems and ovate leaves about 40 mm long with serrated margins, each tooth having a hair-tip. The delicate, shimmering flowers are pink with maroon markings and have 2 tailed petals and a hooded sepal with a spur. Flowering takes place from October to April. Found in deep or dappled shade beside forest streams along the escarpment.

MALVACEAE

Hibiscus engleri (=H. irritans) Wild Hibiscus, Wildehibiskus

This perennial should be handled with extreme caution as it has highly irritant star-shaped hairs which can cause great discomfort to sensitive skins. It is approximately 1 m high with 3–5-lobed leaves with dentate margins. The yellow flowers, 60–70 mm wide, are maroon in the centre with short filaments staggered up the column and a 5-branched style. These striking flowers open in the morning, close up and fade to red by evening. Flowering takes place from December to April. Grows in rocky situations and has been recorded from scattered localities, at various altitudes.

BOMBACACEAE

Adansonia digitata Baobab, Kremetartboom

Because of its remarkable shape this is probably the best-known and most frequently depicted tree in Africa. It is normally 10–15 m high with an extremely stout trunk, thick tapering branches, smooth coppery bark and digitate leaves. The pendent white flowers, up to 200 mm wide, are breath-takingly beautiful with velvety calyx lobes, large crushed-satin petals and numerous showy stamens. Flowering occurs during October and November. The tree is not only spectacular but also utilitarian: a refreshing drink is made from the fruit pulp which contains tartaric acid, the fresh leaves are eaten as a vegetable and the bark provides fibre. This legendary tree is also important in tribal medicine and witchcraft. Confined to hot, open woodland of the northern and central Lowveld.

Greyia radlkoferi

Impatiens sylvicola

Hibiscus engleri (=H. irritans)

Adansonia digitata

STERCULIACEAE

Dombeya cymosa Natal Wild Pear, Natalse Wildepeer

Beautiful in bloom, this distinctive tree graces the autumn landscape. It grows up to 8 m high and the leaves, about 80 mm long, are more or less heart-shaped with serrated margins. The inflorescence is a branched head of fragrant white flowers, about 10 mm wide, which remain on the tree for some time, maturing to yellow and finally brown. Flowering takes place from March to July. Recorded from a few scattered localities of low to medium altitudes, on stream banks and in sheltered ravines. There are some lovely specimens in Crocodile Gorge.

Dombeya pulchra Silver Wild Pear, Blombos

This tree is multi-stemmed and bushy, 2–5 m high and has velvety, rounded, shallowly lobed leaves which are about 120 mm wide with irregularly dentate margins. The upper surface is dark green and the lower silver. The showy, pendent white flowers, with pink or maroon in the centre, are about 25 mm wide and are often held just below the leaves. Flowering takes place from January to May. Found in woodland and on stream banks at low to medium altitudes.

Dombeya rotundifolia Wild Pear, Dombeya, Wildepeer

The Swazi name umBikanyaka means "herald of the new season" and the sight of these flowering trees dotted all over the countryside is a sure indication that spring is on the way. Generally 4–6 m high, it is well-branched, with a pleasing shape and rough, dark brown bark. The rough-textured leaves are more or less circular with irregularly dentate margins. This tree never fails to flower abundantly, producing great clouds of flowers before the new leaves appear. The flowers are about 15 mm wide, with asymmetric petals shaped almost like little windmill blades. They are usually white, but some trees have flowers of a buff-pink hue, while the occasional tree has blooms of a splendid, true rose-pink. Flowering occurs from July to September. The flowers remain on the tree for a few weeks, becoming a warm, light brown, and last for more than a year in a vase. Occurs over a wide range of altitudes over the entire region, usually on rocky hillsides or in open woodland.

Dombeya cymosa

Dombeya pulchra

Dombeya rotundifolia

D. rotundifolia

STERCULIACEAE

Sterculia murex Lowveld Chestnut, Ashtray Tree, Laeveldkastaiing

This fascinating tree is attractive at any time of the year and is endemic to the southern portion of the Transvaal Lowveld, not occurring anywhere else in the world. It grows 6–10 m high and has digitate leaves with soft, velvety leaflets up to 180 mm long. The spring foliage is copper, appearing with or just after the flowers, while the autumn leaves have lovely yellow and bronze hues. The inflorescence is a branched head of pendent yellow flowers with red to maroon markings and the flower, about 20 mm wide, has no petals. The showy, saucer-shaped calyx has 5 to 6 lobes and a waxy texture. Flowering occurs from July to Semptember. The 5-lobed ovary of a single flower develops into a large woody fruit with 1–5 segments, which are up to 150 mm long and copiously covered with thick, hard spines. The segments split open, sometimes forcibly and audibly, and contain large black seeds, up to 30 mm long, which have a delicious nutty flavour and are relished by squirrels, monkeys, baboons and people, who usually roast them on coals. The segments are frequently used as ashtrays but should be handled with care as they have irritant hairs on the inside surface. Restricted to medium altitude, rocky outcrops in the south.

Sterculia rogersii Common Star-chestnut, Gewone Sterkastaiing

This intriguing tree, with its thick, swollen trunk and beautiful bark is sometimes mistaken for a young Baobab. It is 3–5 m high and has a bronze outer bark which peels off the pale, creamy-green inner bark in papery strips. The soft leaves, 30–50 mm long, are 3-lobed and more or less heart-shaped and the flowers are clustered on short lateral shoots. The flower, roughly 20 mm wide, consists of a yellow saucer-shaped calyx with 5 or 6 lobes and is striped with red. The fruit has 1–5 spineless, velvety segments about 50 mm long that harden and become brown as they mature. This is a tree of hot, dry, rocky hillsides and has been recorded from scattered localities at low altitudes.

Sterculia murex   *S. murex*

Sterculia rogersii   *S. rogersii*

OCHNACEAE

Ochna natalitia Mickey Mouse Bush, Natal Plane, Natalrooihout

This charming shrub has a neat shape, pretty flowers and fascinating Mickey Mouse fruits, all these factors combining to make it an asset in a garden. Usually 1–3 m high, it has oblong to oblanceolate leaves with finely serrated margins. The spring foliage is deep copper. The fragrant yellow flowers, 20–30 mm wide, have crinkly petals and dark yellow or orange anthers. Flowering occurs from August to November. Small, roundish black fruits (Mickey Mouse's ears) are borne on a fleshy red base, surrounded by the sepals which have now become red: a colourful picture, and apparently irresistible to birds, who greedily eat the fruits. This interesting plant sometimes has leafy red galls which resemble dwarf, unopened proteas, and are frequently mistaken for the true flower of *Ochna natalitia*. It is relatively common on rocky outcrops and in bushy places over a wide range of altitudes, throughout the entire region.

CLUSIACEAE (=GUTTIFERAE)

Hypericum revolutum Curry Bush, Kerriebos

This bushy shrub, common along streams and forest margins, has a strong curry aroma. It is 2–4 m high with lanceolate leaves about 20 mm long and attractive yellow flowers. They are 40–50 mm wide with spreading petals and numerous yellow stamens. Flowering is irregular and sporadic, throughout the year. Recorded along the whole escarpment.

FLACOURTIACEAE

Oncoba spinosa Snuffbox Tree, Fried Egg Flower, Snuifkalbassie

The woody, dried shells of the fruits of this tree are used as snuffboxes and for ornamental purposes. Generally 3–6 m high, this shrub or tree invariably has a rounded bushy shape. It has sharp spines and glossy, ovate leaves about 60 mm long, with serrated margins. The fragrant "fried-egg" flowers, approximately 60 mm wide, have snow-white petals and a "yolk" of showy yellow stamens. The flat, circular stigma is held above the stamens. Flowering takes place from September to January. The fruit is a woody capsule about 50 mm in diameter, containing small, shiny brown seeds. Recorded from scattered localities in low to medium altitude woodland and on stream banks.

Ochna natalitia

O. natalitia

Hypericum revolutum

Oncoba spinosa

PASSIFLORACEAE

Adenia digitata Bobbejaangif

Although this climber belongs to the granadilla family, its fruits are not edible, being dangerously poisonous. The slender stem is purply-green and climbs by means of tendrils. The variously-lobed leaves are about 80 mm long and the flowers are borne in little clusters. The corolla tube is a slender cream trumpet with maroon markings and is about 15 mm long. Flowering takes place from September to December. The attactive but dangerous, oval red fruits are up to 50 mm long and split into 3 or 4 valves, exposing black seeds in yellow pulp. Ingestion of the fruits could be fatal, and the rootstock is also poisonous. Grows in bushy places, often on rocky outcrops at a wide range of altitudes over the entire region.

BEGONIACEAE

Begonia sonderiana Wild Begonia, Wildebegonia

This elusive plant will probably be found where the trickle of water can be heard nearby, for it grows in deep, damp, forest shade on the mountains. It is a soft, fleshy perennial about 400 mm high with reddish stems and petioles. The asymmetric leaves are obscurely 5-lobed and up to 100 mm long with red veins and irregularly toothed margins. The lustrous, delicate shell-pink flowers are up to 15 mm wide and open from December to March. Recorded from scattered localities along the escarpment.

Begonia sutherlandii Wild Begonia, Wildebegonia

The cheerful flowers of this begonia light up dark, damp places in mountain forests. The fleshy, soft plant is about 300 mm high and the asymmetric leaves, about 100 mm long, are irregularly lobed and toothed. The flowers are bright coral to deep orange and appear from November to March. Recorded from the central and southern escarpment.

Adenia digitata

A. digitata

Begonia sonderiana

Begonia sutherlandii

MELASTOMATACEAE

Dissotis canescens Wild Tibouchina, Wilde Tibouchina

This attractive vlei perennial is often found in association with the yellow vlei orchid, *Eulophia angolensis*, and when flowering simultaneously, they provide a glorious display of colour. The *Dissotis* grows up to 1,5 m high, has short bristly hairs and hard oblong leaves which are about 80 mm long and 3–5-veined from the base. The pretty, warm-pink flowers are about 25 mm wide and have 2 sets of stamens: 5 are short and yellow, the other 5 are longer, pink and articulated, springing out to disperse the ripe pollen. Flowering occurs from December to April. Grows at medium to high altitudes from north to south.

LYTHRACEAE

Galpinia transvaalica Wild Pride-of-India, Transvaal Privet, Transvaalliguster

One of the finest local flowering shrubs, it has crinkly white flowers resembling those of Pride-of-India, which belongs to the same family. It is most rewarding in a garden and, although the flowering period is brief, the flowers are usually borne in profusion, transforming the tree into a white cloud. It grows up to 5 m high and has glossy oval leaves about 40 mm long, with undulate margins. Flowering takes place from December to March. Grows in low altitude woodland in the south.

THYMELAEACEAE

Gnidia caffra (=Lasiosiphon caffer)

This shrublet, about 300 mm high, is particularly striking after fires. It is multi-stemmed, covered with soft hairs and has narrow oval leaves which are up to 30 mm long. The inflorescence is a lax head of shiny yellow flowers, each with minute petals surrounded by 5 conspicuous sepals which are about 5 mm long. The flowering period is mainly from July to September. Found in open grassland in the central and southern areas, generally at medium to high altitudes.

Gnidia kraussiana (=Lasiosiphon kraussii)

This colourful, bushy shrublet with its reddish stems and brilliant yellow flowers is a lovely feature of the spring veld in this region. It is about 300 mm high and has narrow lanceolate leaves about 25 mm long. The superb spherical inflorescence, 30–40 mm wide, is a dense head of small yellow flowers with minute petals and showy sepals. Flowering occurs mainly from August to November. Confined to high altitude grassland in the central and southern regions.

Dissotis canescens

Galpinia transvaalica

Gnidia caffra (=Lasiosiphon caffer)

Gnidia kraussiana (=Lasiosiphon kraussii)

COMBRETACEAE

Because of its large representation, this family is one of the most important components of the Lowveld bush. The combretums are characterised by their 4-winged fruits which often remain on the trees for many months, whereas the terminalias have 2 winged, shield-shaped fruits.

Combretum apiculatum subsp. *apiculatum* Red Bushwillow, Rooiboswilg

A common feature of rocky outcrops, it is 2–8 m high and has oblong to obovate leaves approximately 100 mm long. The tiny, fragrant flowers are borne in profusion on dense spikes about 50 mm long. Flowering takes place from September to January. The russet fruits are about 20 mm long and mature to a dark brown. Widely distributed in low to medium altitude open woodland.

Combretum microphyllum Flame Creeper, Vlamklimop

This most beautiful combretum has brilliant scarlet flowers which provide a marvellous spectacle of colour along the banks of streams and rivers of the Lowveld during spring. It is a vigorous woody scrambler with leaves up to 80 mm long and is sometimes armed with short woody spines. The flowers have minute petals, the colour being provided by the stamens. Flowering takes place from August to November. The red-gold fruits are 25 mm long and mature to a dull brown. Occurs from north to south.

Combretum imberbe Leadwood, Hardekool

This is one of the well-known trees of the Lowveld and is especially common in the Kruger National Park. It is a stately tree about 15 m high. The trunk is usually tall and straight and the distinctive pale grey bark has shallow oblong fissures. The wood is extremely hard, hence the vernacular name. Old weathered logs are highly prized for gardens where they are used as supports for orchids and other plants or left to stand on their own as natural sculptures. They also make most effective pillars. The small leaves are grey-green and about 40 mm long, with undulate margins. Small, fragrant cream flowers are borne in slender spikes about 50 mm long from October to December. The golden fruits, 15 mm long, age to a light brown. Occurring in low to medium altitude woodland, it is sometimes also found along watercourses and in old, dry river beds.

Combretum apiculatum subsp. *apiculatum*

Combretum microphyllum

Combretum imberbe

C. imberbe

COMBRETACEAE

Combretum zeyheri Large-fruited Bushwillow, Raasblaar

The fruits of this combretum are the largest within the genus, being up to 80 mm long, and lend a distinctive, decorative appearance to the fruiting tree. It grows up to 8 m high and has oblong to oval leaves about 80 mm long. The spikes of pale yellow-green flowers are approximately 50 mm long and the flowering time is from August to October. Initially green, the fruits mature and dry to a golden brown. Grows on rocky outcrops and in mixed woodland at low to medium altitudes.

Combretum collinum subsp. *suluense* Weeping Bushwillow, Treurboswilg

This is probably the most common combretum in the Nelspruit area and is 4–10 m high with oblong leaves 100–150 mm long. Tiny, fragrant cream or pale green flowers are borne in plump spikes from August to November. The fruits, around 30 mm long, vary from dull pink to a rich red-brown. Grows at low to medium altitudes in open woodland.

Terminalia sericea Silver Cluster-leaf, Silver Terminalia, Vaalboom

This handsome, shapely tree, with its silver leaves and contrasting dark grey-brown bark, is one of the most striking components of the Lowveld bush and grows almost exclusively on sandy soils. It is usually 4–10 m high and the slender, silky leaves are crowded towards the tips of the branches. The small, creamy-yellow flowers, in spikes about 50 mm long, have an unusual odour, considered by many to be decidedly unpleasant. Flowering takes place from October to December. The buff-pink to rose-red fruits are sometimes parasitised, resulting in tangled, deformed clusters. Widely distributed over the Lowveld, it also occurs on the foothills. It is somewhat more abundant in the south and there are some fine stands near Pretoriuskop in the Kruger National Park.

Terminalia prunioides Lowveld Cluster-leaf, Purple-pod Terminalia, Sterkbos

Although not as shapely as the previous species, this shrub or small tree is magnificent both in full bloom and in fruit. The clustered leaves are darker green, shorter and broader than those of *T. sericea* but the white or creamy-yellow flowers have the same strange odour. Flowering takes place from October to January. The fruits are crimson or purple, making the tree conspicuous and easy to identify in autumn and winter. Scattered over the whole Lowveld, in dry, open woodland.

Combretum zeyheri

Combretum collinum subsp. *suluense*

Terminalia sericea

Terminalia prunioides

APIACEAE (=UMBELLIFERAE)

Steganotaenia araliacea Carrot Tree, Geelwortelboom

Belonging to the same family as the domestic vegetable, this tree has a strong carrot-aroma and the family affinity is evident also in the inflorescence and fruit. The tree grows up to 6 m high and has grey-green bark which peels off in papery strips. The pinnate leaves, crowded at the tips of the stubby twigs, are about 200 mm long with 5–7 soft, pale green leaflets which are ovate, with conspicuously serrated margins and long, tapering tips. Tiny, pale yellow flowers are borne in branched, spherical heads up to 200 mm in diameter, before the new leaves appear. The flowering tree has a soft, delicate appearance which tempers the harsh, rocky hillsides from August to October. The flat, sticky fruit is oblong and about 8 mm long, with the seed encircled by a narrow, compressed wing. Grows on wooded rocky slopes, generally at low to medium altitudes.

OLEACEAE

Jasminum stenolobum Wild Jasmine, Wildejasmyn

This scrambler, covered with soft hairs, has long woody stems and usually grows on rocky outcrops. The leaves are generally broad lanceolate to ovate and 20–30 mm long. The beautiful white flowers, about 20 mm wide, are red on the outside and have a delightful fragrance. The red buds and white blooms give the flowering bush a gay, colourful air. Flowering takes place from August to October. The fruits are twin berries, ripening to a burnished black, each lobe 8–10 mm in diameter. Occasionally only one half develops. Recorded from scattered localities at low to medium altitudes. It is similar to *Jasminum multipartitum* but the latter is less hairy.

Steganotaenia araliacea

S. araliacea

Jasminum stenolobum

J. stenolobum

ERICACEAE

Erica cerinthoides var. *cerinthoides* Red Hairy Heath, Rooihaartjie

Although the main representation of ericas is in the Cape, where they form an important component of the fynbos, there are a few in the Transvaal region, mainly along the Drakensberg escarpment. Red Hairy Heath has the largest and most striking flowers of the local ericas and is relatively easy to identify. It grows approximately 400 mm high and has small narrow leaves about 6 mm long. The clustered flowers are generally scarlet but may be soft rose-pink or white. The hairy corolla tube is slightly constricted at both ends and is 20–35 mm long. The short lobes are somewhat spreading and occasionally reflexed. When out hiking in the mountains in late summer, it is always a joy to find these beautiful flowers amongst the rocks. Recorded from the central and southern escarpment.

Erica drakensbergensis Drakensberg Heath, Drakensbergse Heide

Probably the largest erica in this area, it grows 1–2 m high and has numerous narrow little leaves 2–4 mm long. Tiny, pendent white bells, 3–4 mm long, are borne in profusion along the branches. The corolla tube narrows towards the apex and the short lobes are recurved. The stamens and style protrude, bearing dark brown anthers and stigma. The flowering period is erratic, herbarium specimens having been collected for every month of the year. Grows in scrubby grassland and on forest margins on the central and southern escarpment.

Erica woodii Heath, Heide

This charming shrublet is normally 200–300 mm high and has short sparse hairs. The narrow leaves, with reflexed margins, are about 3 mm long. The pendent pink flowers are bell-shaped and about 2 mm long, narrowing only slightly towards the apex. The lobes are straight, only slightly outspread at the tips. The anthers are brown and the protruding round stigma is red. Flowering takes place mainly from February to July, but flowers are occasionally seen as late as November. Restricted to rocky grassland on the central and southern escarpment.

Erica cerinthoides var. *cerinthoides*

E. cerinthoides var. *cerinthoides*

Erica drakensbergensis

Erica woodii

LOGANIACEAE

Strychnos madagascariensis Spineless Monkey Orange, Botterklapper

Striking when in fruit, this widely distributed tree is 3–6 m high with leathery, blue-green, oval leaves about 80 mm long. Clusters of small, yellow-green flowers are borne from August to November. The spherical fruit, 60–80 mm in diameter, is blue-green, ripening to yellow, with a thick, woody shell, and decorates the tree throughout winter into spring. Grows in low to medium altitude, open woodland and on rocky outcrops, very often on sandy soils.

Strychnos spinosa Green Monkey Orange, Suurklapper, Groenklapper

Also 'widely distributed, this strychnos is 3–6 m high, with smooth, glossy, dark green leaves about 70 mm long, borne on short hard shoots that often end in sharp spines. Clustered, tiny green flowers appear from October to January. The decorative, shiny dark green fruit is 70–100 mm in diameter. A fruiting specimen, without its foliage, is a splendid sight. Occurs at low to medium altitudes in sandy or rocky, open woodland.

Although the pulp around the seeds of the 2 species of Strychnos featured here is widely reputed to be edible, it is not advisable to eat it as cases of toxicity in humans have occured.

GENTIANACEAE

Sebaea grandis

A dainty, pretty perennial about 200 mm high. The 4-angled stem has a narrow wing along each edge and the lanceolate leaves are 20–40 mm long. The flowers, cream to yellow, are roughly 30 mm wide, with 5 broad, pointed lobes and the narrow calyx lobes are winged. Flowering takes place during January and February. Generally found in open grassland of the central and southern mountains and foothills.

Nymphoides thunbergiana Yellow Water Lily, Geelwaterlelie

It is always a pleasant surprise to find this charming aquatic perennial in mountain pools, for it is not plentiful anywhere. It has a rooted rhizome and long, slender stems. The almost circular leaves, about 100 mm in diameter, are deeply notched at the base and lie flat on the water's surface. Small yellow flowers, about 30 mm wide, appear in clusters just above the surface and are covered with coarse hairs. Flowering takes place from October to April. Found in stagnant pools or slow-moving water, along the escarpment.

Strychnos madagascariensis

Strychnos spinosa

Sebaea grandis

Nymphoides thunbergiana

APOCYNACEAE

Members of this family include the well-known Frangipani and Oleander and the leaves are generally opposite or whorled. Many produce latex and some of them, like the Oleander, are extremely poisonous.

Acokanthera rotundata (=*A. schimperi* var. *rotundata*) Round-leaved Poison Bush, Rondeblaargifboom

The sap of all the trees within this genus is very toxic and has, in some cases, been used as arrow poison. This particular acokanthera is a bushy shrub or tree 3–4 m high with hard leathery leaves which are glossy dark green above and paler below. They are 50–60 mm long, broad and oval or almost circular and have a short, sharp, spine-like tip. Small fragrant flowers, about 8 mm wide, are borne in dense inflorescences. The corolla tube is red and the asymmetric lobes white. Flowering takes place from August to March. The round to oblong, fleshy fruit is dark red or purple and up to 20 mm in diameter. The fruit and all parts of the plant must be regarded as toxic. Recorded from scattered localities, on rocky places, in dry woodland of medium altitudes.

Tabernaemontana elegans Toad Tree, Paddaboom

In full fruit in a garden, this small tree is bound to be a conversation piece. Its fruits are thought to resemble toads, hence the common name. It is generally 3–4 m high, but grows up to 10 m in forest. It produces a sticky latex and has deeply fissured yellow-grey bark.The oblong to oval leaves are 100–200 mm long and the delicately perfumed white flowers, 15–20 mm wide, have 5 narrow, S-shaped corolla lobes. Flowering takes place from November to January. The intriguing, paired fruits are nearly round and about 50 mm wide, with blue-green skin covered with white, warty knobs. The fruits split open and expose black seeds in a sweet, bright orange pulp which is eaten by birds, animals and humans. The latex is used as a styptic to halt bleeding and also as a bird lime. Found in moist, low-lying evergreen forest and on the banks of streams, and has been recorded from a few localities in the northern and southeastern regions.

Acokanthera rotundata (=A. schimperi var. *rotundata)*

A. rotundata

Tabernaemontana elegans

T. elegans

APOCYNACEAE

Adenium multiflorum (=A. obesum var. *multiflorum)* Impala Lily, Impalalelie

In full bloom this striking succulent shrub provides welcome colour in the drab winter landscape and is a popular photographic subject of visitors to the Kruger National Park. Shingwedzi Camp has some exceptionally fine specimens. It grows up to 2 m high with a swollen stem, fleshy branches and oblong to ovate, undulate leaves up to 100 mm long. The magnificent flowers, about 50 mm wide, have pointed white lobes with crinkly red margins and red stripes in the throat. Flowering takes place from May to September. The twin, cylindrical fruits are 120 mm long and joined at the base. The seeds have silky hairs for wind dispersal. The sap is toxic and has been used as a fish poison and also as arrow poison. Grows in sandy or rocky woodland or open grassland in the hot, low-lying regions, from north to south.

Adenium swazicum Summer Impala Lily, Somerimpalalelie

This dwarf *Adenium* is usually less than 300 mm high with leaves similar to those of the Impala Lily, but shorter and narrower. The beautiful flowers vary from soft shades of pink to rose-red and maroon. They have broad, slightly pointed lobes and open from January to May. Fruits resemble those of the previous species. Grows in the hot, dry Lowveld in open or lightly wooded grassland. Recorded mainly in the Kruger National Park, from north to south.

Pachypodium saundersii Kudu Lily, Koedoelelie

This impressive succulent shrub resembles the Impala Lily but differs in having slender, sharp spines along the branches. Usually less than 1 m high, it has a massive, swollen, almost grotesque stem, with a few rapidly tapering branches and silver-grey bark. The glossy oblong leaves are undulate and 60–70 mm long. The pretty flowers are white, flushed with pink and are borne from April to June. The slender, cylindrical twin fruits are about 100 mm long and split open, releasing numerous seeds with tufts of fine, silky hairs. Recorded from scattered localities at low to medium altitudes and invariably associated with rocky outcrops.

Adenium multiflorum (=A. obesum var. *multiflorum)*

Adenium swazicum

Pachypodium saundersii

P. saundersii

PERIPLOCACEAE

Raphionacme hirsuta

An attractive little perennial up to 100 mm high, producing latex and with fleshy stems. The velvety, ovate leaves are up to 20 mm long and the flowers up to 10 mm wide. In addition to 5 oblong corolla lobes, which are mauve or purple, they have a domed corona of 5 converging white lobes. Flowering takes place from July to November. Found in open grassland on the central and southern mountains and foothills.

ASCLEPIADACEAE

In this family, the leaves are generally opposite or whorled. In addition to 5 corolla lobes, the flowers have a 5-lobed corona and the stamens are united into a column.

Xysmalobium acerateoides Butterscotch Plant

The flowers of this beautiful perennial have a distinct, delectable butterscotch aroma. It is a sprawling plant with radiating, procumbent stems up to 400 mm long, has short rough hairs and produces latex. The erect, lanceolate leaves are up to 70 mm long, with inrolled margins. The dense spherical inflorescence is 20–25 mm in diameter, with creamy-white flowers which are borne from October to January. Grows in open, rocky grassland on the southern escarpment.

Xysmalobium undulatum Bitterhout, Bitterwortel

This splendid robust perennial, up to 1 m high, is covered with fine hairs and produces copious amounts of latex. The hard, lanceolate leaves are up to 200 mm long and have undulate margins. The inflorescence is round and 40–50 mm in diameter, consisting of attractive flowers that are cream, pink and yellow-green. The corolla lobes are fringed with fluffy white hairs. Flowering takes place from October to February. The inflated fruits, up to 100 mm long, are covered with soft, curly pink hairs and are most attractive. Grows in open grassland on the southern mountains and foothills.

Raphionacme hirsuta

Xysmalobium acerateoides

Xysmalobium undulatum

X. undulatum

ASCLEPIADACEAE

Schizoglossum robustum var. *pubiflorum*

This velvety perennial is stiff and erect and grows up to 1 m high. It produces latex and has narrow undulate leaves approximately 30 mm long. The clustered flowers, about 15 mm wide, have dull purple corolla lobes reflexed from the white corona which has slender extensions, rather like the tentacles of a miniature octopus. Flowering takes place from November to March. Grows in medium to high altitude grassland and has been recorded only in the south.

Pachycarpus campanulatus

The large, pendent flowers of this slender *pachycarpus* are delightful, and most distinctive. The plant grows up to 600 mm high and produces latex. It is covered with short bristly hairs and has linear leaves up to 120 mm long. The wide, bell-shaped flowers are creamy or golden-beige, roughly 30 mm wide, with broad corolla lobes and short, blunt corona lobes which are yellow and dark maroon. Flowering takes place from November to February. Grows in open grassland on the central and southern mountains.

Pachycarpus transvaalensis

Robust and about 500 mm high, it has short rough hairs and produces latex, and the oblong, undulate leaves are about 100 mm long. The flattened flower buds are somewhat mundane but they open out into magnificent, colourful flowers about 20 mm wide. The yellow-orange corolla lobes have maroon stripes and the striking corona has plump maroon lobes, while the staminal column is yellow and white. Flowering takes place during November and December. Grows in grassland on the southern mountains and foothills.

Pachycarpus validus Giant Milkweed, Grootmelkbos

The enormous fruits of this sturdy milkweed always catch the eye. It grows up to 800 mm high, produces latex and has leathery undulate leaves up to 150 mm long. The clustered, pendent flowers are green, yellow and pink, with the corolla lobes reflexed from the corona. Flowering takes place from November to January. Only 1–3 fruits develop per stem. They are oval and leathery, 100–120 mm long, with prominent peaked ridges and contain numerous seeds with tufts of silky hairs. Recorded at varying altitudes over the entire region, in open or lightly wooded grassland.

Schizoglossum robustum var. *pubiflorum*

Pachycarpus campanulatus

Pachycarpus transvaalensis

Pachycarpus validus

ASCLEPIADACEAE

Asclepias physocarpa Milkweed, Melkbos

The inflated fruits of this perennial pop audibly underfoot, to the great delight of children, who find them irresistible. Sparsely branched, it grows 1–2 m high, produces copious amounts of latex and has narrow leaves about 80 mm long. The pink and white flowers are borne in clusters from October to March. Almost spherical, the fruits are about 70 mm in diameter and are covered with soft curved bristles. They contain small black seeds, each with a tuft of silky hairs. Grows in damp grassland and vleis over virtually the entire Lowveld and escarpment.

Asclepias velutina

This charming little velvety perennial, 50–100 mm high, is easily overlooked in the veld. It produces latex and the linear leaves are up to 50 mm long, with inrolled margins. The dainty flowers have palest pink, reflexed corolla lobes and the corona has erect, pointed lobes with rose-pink tips. Flowering takes place from June to October. Grows in mountain grassland, in the south.

Sarcostemma viminale Melktou

This vigorous, succulent scrambler climbs into and drapes itself over surrounding vegetation and produces copious amounts of latex. The leafless fleshy stems are 5–6 mm in diameter and can become several meters long. The fragrant little flowers, about 10 mm wide, are borne in attractive clusters. The corolla has narrow, yellow-green lobes and the compact, double corona is creamy-white. Flowering takes place from October to May. The cylindrical twin fruits are about 80 mm long. They split open to release flattish brown seeds, each with an inverted parachute of silky hairs to facilitate wind dispersal. Occurs at various altitudes in a variety of rocky and bushy habitats over the entire region.

Asclepias physocarpa

Asclepias velutina

Sarcostemma viminale

S. viminale

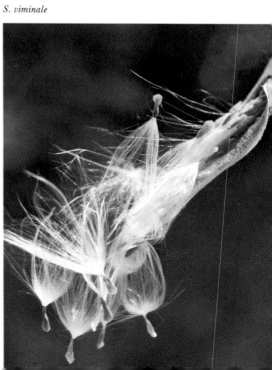

ASCLEPIADACEAE

Ceropegias are climbers or scramblers with opposite leaves and delightful flowers. The corolla tube, inflated at the base, widens near the apex, dividing into 5 lobes which, in the species illustrated here, are united at their tips, forming open little cage-like structures. The corona, situated inside the tube, is not visible. The slender twin fruits are approximately 100 mm long.

Ceropegia ampliata Bushman's Pipe, Boesmanpypblom

A vigorous succulent scrambler with a smooth, fleshy stem that produces roots from nodes that come into contact with soil. Minute heart-shaped leaves, 2–3 mm long, drop off at an early stage. The plump white flower is about 50 mm long and has yellow-green lobes. Flowering takes place during March and April. This rare plant has been recorded from the south in rocky woodland at medium altitudes.

Ceropegia meyeri

This climber, covered with soft hairs, has a slender twining stem and leaves which are more or less heart-shaped and 20–50 mm long. The beautiful, bottle-shaped flowers, 40–50 mm long, are white with maroon or purple markings and the hairy, deep purple lobes form a short, squat cage. Flowering takes place from December to March. Recorded from the central and southern areas where it grows in bushy, rocky places and open woodland, at medium altitudes.

Ceropegia racemosa subsp. *setifera*

A slender twining plant with velvety, somewhat ovate leaves which are 40–60 mm long. The flowers, 30–50 mm long, are creamy-green with faint maroon markings and bright yellow-green lobes with maroon at the tips. Flowering takes place from November to February. Occurs in rocky, bushy places at medium to high altitudes in the central and southern regions.

Riocreuxia torulosa

This vigorous, velvety scrambler has a long twining stem and heart-shaped leaves 50–100 mm long. The charming little white flowers, about 16 mm long, have slender orange lobes which form a very narrow cage. Flowering takes place from December to February. It grows in bushy places and on forest margins along the escarpment and foothills.

Ceropegia ampliata

Ceropegia meyeri

Ceropegia racemosa subsp. *setifera*

Riocreuxia torulosa

ASCLEPIADACEAE

Brachystelma gracile

Very easily overlooked in the veld, this slender, grass-like perennial is up to 600 mm high with narrow leaves up to 80 mm long. The ethereal pendent flowers, 10–15 mm long, have grey-green, threadlike corolla lobes united at the apex to form a loose, open cage. The corona is small and inconspicuous. Flowering takes place from October to January. The narrow, cylindrical twin fruits are about 100 mm long. Grows on partially shaded rocky outcrops and has been recorded only in the south, at medium altitudes.

Huernia hystrix

A dwarf succulent, up to 100 mm high, with leafless, 5-angled stems. The captivating flower, cream with maroon stripes, is approximately 40 mm wide. The bowl-shaped corolla tube flattens out into a wide brim which is shallowly 5-lobed and covered with soft fleshy bristles. The small corona is maroon. Flowering takes place from November to February. The erect twin fruits are up to 100 mm long. Found on rocky outcrops in open woodland at low to medium altitudes in the central and southern areas.

Stapelia gigantea (=S. nobilis) Giant Stapelia, Reuseaasblom

This velvety succulent has leafless 4-angled stems up to 200 mm high. The enormous malodorous flowers attract flies and bluebottles: the Afrikaans "Aasblom" means "carrion flower!". The spectacular 5-lobed flower, generally 200–300 mm wide, looks like a starfish. It has silky hairs and is creamy-yellow, with irregular maroon ridges and the tiny corona is maroon. Flowering takes place in autumn. The erect twin fruits are maroon and velvety, up to 200 mm long. Grows in scattered localities in the central and southern areas, in open granitic woodland of low to medium altitudes.

Stapelia leendertziae Bell Stapelia, Rooiaasblom, Aasklok

A velvety succulent about 150 mm high with leafless 4-angled stems. The striking bell-shaped flower is deep burgundy, about 100 mm long and has 5 short triangular lobes with recurved tips. The outer surface is smooth, the inner velvety with fine ridges. It also has a strong carrion odour and normally flowers in midsummer. Grows on wooded rocky outcrops in a few scattered localities in the central and southern regions.

Brachystelma gracile

Huernia hystrix

Stapelia gigantea (=S. nobilis)

Stapelia leendertziae

CONVOLVULACEAE

Some plants in this family, of the genus *Ipomoea*, are extensively cultivated in various parts of the world e.g. Sweet Potato and Morning Glory.

Ipomoea albivenia Wild Cotton, Wildekatoen

A vigorous, velvety scrambler/climber with heart-shaped leaves up to 120 mm long which are conspicuously felty below. About 50 mm wide, the attractive funnel-shaped flowers are crinkly white with pale pink or yellow in the throat. They open during the night and die back by noon. Flowering takes place from December to February. When the fruit capsules burst open they release seeds embedded in fluffy white "cotton wool". Widely distributed at low to medium altitudes, on rocky outcrops and in open woodland.

Ipomoea cairica Messina Creeper, Wild Morning Glory

This vigorous climber has long slender stems several metres long, which drape themselves over the surrounding vegetation. The palmately lobed leaves are up to 20 mm long and the pretty, mauve flowers have a deeper flush in the throat. They are approximately 40 mm in diameter and flowering generally takes place from February to April. It is often cultivated and has also been reported as a weed. Widespread at low to medium altitudes and often grows in riverine bush.

Ipomoea crassipes Wild Morning Glory

The beautiful, deep mauve or magenta flowers of this luxuriant, trailing perennial provide great carpets of colour in summer. The stems are long and slender and the variable leaves up to 60 mm long. The flowers are about 50 mm wide and are borne in profusion from November to March. Widely distributed at various altitudes in grassland and disturbed soil, and often found on road verges.

Turbina oblongata

Its erect leaves make this shaggy scrambler easy to identify. It has an enormous rootstock about 500 × 100 mm in extent. The more or less oblong leaves are 40–100 mm long and the handsome flowers, about 60 mm wide, are generally a deep, rich magenta. Flowering takes place from November to February. When food is scarce the rootstock can be utilised: it is ground up and mixed with sour milk. Occurs at various altitudes and is sometimes found on road verges where it benefits from the camber run-off moisture. Recorded mainly from the central and southern areas.

Ipomoea albivenia

Ipomoea cairica

Ipomoea crassipes

Turbina oblongata

BORAGINACEAE

Trichodesma physaloides Chocolate Creams, Chocolate Bells, Sjokoladeklokkies

This bushy shrublet is as enchanting as its vernacular names, which refer to the colours of the pendent blooms. It is about 600 mm high, with numerous purply-brown stems and broad lanceolate leaves up to 60 mm long. The delightful white, bell-shaped flowers turn brown at the edges and are borne in profusion in veld that has been burnt. Flowering takes place from August to October. Grows in open grassland along the central and southern escarpment and foothills.

VERBENACEAE

Chascanum latifolium var. *glabrescens*

An attractive shrublet up to 500 mm high with oval to obovate leaves up to 70 mm long. The flowers, about 15 mm long, are palest pink, almost white, with reflexed lateral lobes. Flowering takes place from August to December. Recorded from the south, in mountain grassland.

◆*Lantana camara* Lantana
PROCLAIMED WEED

This rampant weed is a prickly scrambler with round, compact inflorescences about 30 mm wide, varying from white, yellow and pink to orange. The flowering period is erratic. The purple berries are eaten by birds and animals, thus assuring wide dispersal of the seed. This troublesome pest was introduced from Tropical America as a horticultural subject and has escaped into the wild, forming impenetrable thickets which are extremely difficult to eradicate. Found at various altitudes on forest margins, the banks of streams and in bushy areas.

Clerodendrum triphyllum

A bright, bushy little shrub 150–500 mm high with narrow oval to oblong leaves which are 20–40 mm long and are borne singly, in pairs or whorled. The pretty, dark blue to purple flowers have 5 corolla lobes and arching stamens and style. The flowers are about 15 mm long and open from August to March. Grows at medium to high altitudes in open or lightly wooded grassland.

Trichodesma physaloides

Chascanum latifolium var. *glabrescens*

Lantana camara

Clerodendrum triphyllum

VERBENACEAE

Holmskioldia tettensis Cups-and-saucers, Wild Parasol Flower, Wildeparasolblom

This colourful shrub is just as successful and showy in a garden as the cultivated holmskioldias. It grows 2–4 m high with ovate leaves about 30 mm long and most attractive flowers. The warm-pink saucer-shaped calyx has shallow, rounded lobes and the stamens and style protrude from the purple corolla which drops off at an early stage. Flowering usually takes place from December to March. Grows on hot, dry, rocky outcrops in a few scattered localities in the central and southern areas, at various altitudes.

LAMIACEAE (=LABIATAE)

Many members of this family are aromatic e.g. mint, rosemary and salvia, and they frequently have 4-angled stems, while the leaves are generally opposite or whorled.

Leonotis dysophylla Wild Dagga, Klipdagga, Wildedagga

This vernacular name, Wild Dagga, is a complete misnomer, for the plant is totally innocuous, with no narcotic properties. The name *Leonotis* means "lion's ear", and its origin can be seen in the shape and furry texture of the flowers. This dramatic plant has stems 2–3 m high with more or less oval leaves and conspicuous, compact clusters of brilliant orange flowers, borne from January to May. Forms colonies in grassland and on rocky outcrops at various altitudes.

Pycnostachys urticifolia Hedgehog Bush, Blue Boys

These spiny, hedgehog inflorescences, with their bright, cornflower-blue blooms, are most distinctive in the local vleis, especially in late summer. This shrub grows up to 3 m high and has ovate leaves up to 80 mm long. The inflorescences have pale pink buds providing a soft contrast to the flowers, and the calyxes have spiny teeth up to 10 mm long. Flowering takes place from October to May. Grows in damp places, generally at low to medium altitudes, and recorded from north to south.

Rabdosia calycina

This sparsely branched shrub is about 1 m high and has broadly ovate leaves about 60 mm long, with dentate margins. The inflorescence has tiny velvety flowers in delicate shades of pink and mauve, which are 2-lipped and about 10 mm long. Flowering takes place from February to May. Generally found in the cool, rocky, misty grassland of the central and southern mountains.

Holmskioldia tettensis

Leonotis dysophylla

Pycnostachys urticifolia

Rabdosia calycina

LAMIACEAE

Plectranthus fruticosus

This aromatic shrub is a good garden subject, particularly when massed. It grows to 2 m high and the ovate leaves, up to 100 mm long, have coarse, irregular teeth. The branched inflorescence has numerous mauve to purple, 2-lipped flowers about 10 mm long, with small purple dots on the upper lip. Flowering takes place from February to May. Grows at medium to high altitudes in forests and bushy places of the central and southern regions.

Plectranthus verticillatus Gossip

This charming perennial is an outstanding ground cover, spreading just as rapidly as gossip does! It is semi-succulent and roots at the nodes. The soft, fleshy leaves are almost circular, with coarsely dentate margins and are often purple below. The inflorescence is about 100 mm long and the dainty, 2-lipped flowers are white or palest mauve, with minute purple speckles. Flowering takes place from February to June. It favours light shade and is found on rocky outcrops at various altitudes in the central and southern regions.

Tetradenia riparia (=Iboza riparia) Mountain Mist, Ginger Bush, Wildesalie, Watersalie

In full bloom this aromatic shrub provides misty clouds of delicate colour in a drab winter landscape. It grows up to 2 m high, depending on its habitat and has brittle, semi-succulent branches. The velvety leaves, 30–60 mm long and more or less oval, are lobed at the base and have large blunt teeth on the margins. The tiny male and female flowers are borne on separate plants and the colour varies from white to palest pink or mauve. The male inflorescence is a graceful, lax spray with flowers about 3 mm long and the more compact female inflorescence has smaller flowers, about 2 mm long. This shrub flowers briefly but gloriously, from June to August. It grows at low to medium altitudes in a wide variety of habitats, ranging from dry rocky outcrops to the banks of streams. Recorded from numerous localities, from north to south.

Plectranthus fruticosus

Plectranthus verticillatus

Tetradenia riparia (= Iboza riparia) ♂

T. riparia (♀)

LAMIACEAE
Hemizygia transvaalensis
In spring and early summer this charming shrub provides whole fields of colour, conspicuous in burnt veld. It is sticky and aromatic and grows up to 600 mm high. The ovate leaves, about 20 mm long, have finely serrated margins. The branched inflorescence has showy pink bracts and 2-lipped pink flowers with maroon calyxes. Flowering takes place from August to December. Found in open or lightly wooded grassland on the central and southern escarpment and foothills.

Becium obovatum var. galpinii
A soft, subtly hued shrublet about 300 mm high, with narrowly oval, grey-green leaves which are about 40 mm long and have minute, irregular teeth on the margins. The conical inflorescence elongates as the pretty, 2-lipped flowers open. They are pale mauve, about 10 mm long and the upper lip is lobed and striped, with a frilly margin. Flowering takes place from August to November. Occurs in open or lightly wooded grassland on the central and southern mountains and foothills.

SOLANACEAE
◆Solanum mauritianum Bug Tree, Bug Weed, Luisboom
PROCLAIMED WEED
Visitors to the Lowveld and escarpment would be forgiven for regarding this as an indigenous plant: it seems ubiquitous! It is a woolly shrub or tree 2–5 m high with ovate leaves and leaf-like stipules. Mauve flowers are borne from July to October and the yellow berries, about 10 mm in diameter, contain numerous seeds which are relished by birds, thus assuring dispersal. Native to Asia, it is now probably beyond control in this area and can be found in planted and natural forests, along the banks of streams, in lands and on road verges, at various altitudes.

SCROPHULARIACEAE
Sutera grandiflora Sutera

In its natural state this sutera tends to become straggly and flops around unless supported by other vegetation. However, if it is regularly trimmed, it can be very pretty in a garden. It is 600–800 mm high, with narrow oval leaves up to 30 mm long and shimmering mauve flowers up to 20 mm wide. Occasionally a plant with white flowers will be found. Flowering is irregular. Grows in rocky grassland or sheltered forest margins of medium to high altitudes in the central and southern districts.

Hemizygia transvaalensis

Becium obovatum var. *galpinii*

Solanum mauritianum

Sutera grandiflora

SCROPHULARIACEAE

The plants featured on this page are all parasites which attack the roots of various grasses and herbs.

Cycnium adonense Ink Plant, Handkerchief Plant, Inkblom

Often flowering prolifically after fires, these plants are conspicuous white blobs in the bare black veld, like hankies or tissues tossed about carelessly. The delicate white flowers turn inky-blue with age or when damaged. This ground-hugging perennial is 100–200 mm high and has oval leaves with serrated margins and short rough hairs. The flowers are about 50 mm wide and flowering takes place from September to November. Herbarium specimens are pitch black. Grows in open grassland at various altitudes over the entire region.

Cycnium racemosum

Its stunning, clear rose-pink flowers make this one of the most handsome parasites found in the region. It grows up to 600 mm high and has short rough hairs and lanceolate leaves up to 80 mm long, with coarsely serrated margins. The fragrant flowers, about 40 mm wide, have a patch of white in the throat. Flowering takes place from December to March. Herbarium specimens dry black. Grows in open grassland on the central and southern mountains and foothills.

Harveya huttonii

The superb, pale pink flowers of this erect perennial brighten rocky places on the escarpment. Generally 200–300 mm high, it is covered with short rough hairs and has tiny narrow leaves about 10 mm long. The flowers, about 40 mm wide, have 5 irregularly toothed corolla lobes and are yellow in the throat. Flowering occurs from December to February. Recorded from scattered localities along the length of the escarpment.

Striga elegans Witchweed, Scarlet Pimpernel, Rooiblom, Rooibossie

Although closely related to another striga which is a pest in mealie lands, this striking plant is innocuous as it parasitises wild grasses. It is about 20 mm high with very rough short hairs and narrow leaves 20–40 mm long. The close-set flowers are brilliant, almost iridescent scarlet with yellow in the throat and on the lower surface of the corolla lobes. Flowering occurs from November to May. Grows in sunny grassland at various altitudes.

Cycnium adonense

Cycnium racemosum

Harveya huttonii

Striga elegans

SCROPHULARIACEAE

Graderia scabra Wild Pentstemon

This is one of the loveliest spring plants in the region. It is bushy, about 600 mm high with short rough hairs and lanceolate to oval leaves which are about 30 mm long with a few coarse teeth on the margins. The beautiful, soft pink flowers, about 25 mm wide, are clustered along the stems and are usually borne from September to November. Grows in lightly shaded grassland or on rocky outcrops at medium to high altitudes in the central and southern districts.

Buttonia superba

The flowers of this rare parasitic climber are superb. The leaves, 10–15 mm long, are deeply divided into 3–5 narrow lobes. The dark pink flowers, up to 60 mm wide, have prominent maroon ridges on the lower lobe, called nectar guides, for they guide and entice visiting insects into the throat, to the nectar. Flowering takes place from September to March. This climber attacks the roots of various herbs and grasses. It has been recorded from the area around Blyde River Canyon and Mariepskop and also from the southern Kruger National Park.

SELAGINACEAE

Hebenstretia dura

This delightful shrub is restricted to rocky places in the mountains. It is multi-stemmed, about 600 mm high with crowded, slender leaves about 30 mm long. The inflorescences are dense and compact, approximately 50 mm long, and each small white flower has a conspicuous tomato-red splash. Flowering is irregular: there is a herbarium specimen for practically every month of the year. Recorded from scattered localities along the length of the escarpment.

Tetraselago nelsonii

One of the finest blue-flowering perennials in this region, it is about 500 mm high with narrow leaves up to 15 mm long, crowded in little clusters. The slightly domed inflorescences are branched and about 60 mm wide with masses of small 4–5-lobed flowers varying from blue to mauve. Flowering takes place from December to June. Found only on the escarpment, where it grows in open or lightly wooded, rocky grassland.

Graderia scabra

Buttonia superba

Hebenstretia dura

Tetraselago nelsonii

BIGNONIACEAE
Kigelia africana Sausage Tree, Worsboom

With its splendid flowers and large sausage-shaped fruits, this tree is well-known to tourists in the Kruger National Park. At Tshokwane resting place, north of Skukuza, a litttle tea-room has been built around the trunk of a Sausage Tree. It grows to about 10 m high and the pinnate leaves are about 300 mm long, with hard, brittle leaflets. The beautiful burgundy, trumpet-shaped flowers, about 80 mm long, have an unusual, haunting fragrance and are visited by sunbirds from dawn to dusk: they often peck a hole in the back of the flower, taking a short cut to the copious nectar supply. In full bloom during August and September, the tree is a remarkable sight. The large pendent fruits are up to 500 mm long and weigh up to 4 kg. It is restricted to the hot, low-lying region and often grows on the banks of streams.

◆ *Jacaranda mimosifolia* Jacaranda, Jakaranda
INTRODUCED

This tree grows to about 10 m high and has bipinnate leaves and delicate mauve flowers borne in dense sprays from September to January. It was introduced from tropical South America as a horticultural subject and has been used to great effect as a street tree e.g. in Pretoria and Barberton. Whereas it is not yet a major problem on the highveld, it has become widely naturalised in the Lowveld and is evident along the banks of rivers, one of the worst infestations being along the lower reaches of the Elands River, where it threatens the natural vegetation.

PEDALIACEAE
Ceratotheca triloba Wild Foxglove, Vingerhoedblom

An aromatic shrub up to 2 m high with broadly oval or 3-lobed leaves which are about 50 mm long with bluntly serrated margins. The "foxglove" flowers are delicate pink or mauve, about 60 mm long, with maroon pin-stripes inside the throat and down the lower lobe. Flowering takes place from December to January. Recorded from numerous localities in a variety of habitats and at various altitudes.

Kigelia africana

K. africana

Jacaranda mimosifolia

Ceratotheca triloba

PEDALIACEAE

Dicerocaryum zanguebarium subsp. *zanguebarium*   Devil's Thorn,
  Boot Protector, Beesdubbeltjie, Seepbossie

This prostrate plant is at once beautiful, dangerous and useful: it has charming flowers, fruits which are harmful to animals and barefoot humans and yet it is also used as a soap substitute. The leaves are irregularly lobed and the warm-pink flowers have a few red or maroon stripes. Flowering takes place from November to January. The flattish fruits have 2 hard erect spines which are viciously sharp. If the plant is immersed in water overnight, the resultant mucilaginous jelly can be used as soap or shampoo: merely handling the plant leaves one's hands soapy and slimy. Occurs at various altitudes, mainly low to medium, in sandy or rocky grassland and disturbed soil such as road verges.

GESNERIACEAE

This family provides some of the world's most popular pot plants, such as Gloxinia, African Violet and *Streptocarpus*.

Streptocarpus cyaneus

This soft perennial is tucked away in damp, rocky places in forest shade, often near waterfalls. It has velvety oblong leaves about 200 mm long with veins depressed on the upper surface. The lax inflorescence has 1–6 beautiful flowers, about 30 mm long, in shades of pink or mauve, with darker streaks on the lobes and yellow in the throat. Flowering takes place from October to March. Widely recorded from the central and southern escarpment and foothills.

Streptocarpus dunnii Olifantsoor

The brilliant flowers and single, enormous, oblong leaf make it easy to identify this singular plant. The velvety leaf, up to 600 mm long, has the midrib and veins deeply depressed above. The dense inflorescence has numerous coral to deep orange-red flowers up to 30 mm long. Flowering takes place from November to February. This magnificent plant grows in rock crevices and amongst boulders, high up on the southern mountains.

Streptocarpus galpinii

This tiny plant, with its royal purple flowers, nestles in rock crevices and on shaded rock ledges. It has a few oblong leaves about 100 mm long and the flowers, up to 20 mm wide, have a distinctive, triangular white patch in the throat. Flowering takes place from December to March. Recorded from the central and southern mountains.

Dicerocaryum zanguebarium subsp. *zanguebarium*

Streptocarpus cyaneus

Streptocarpus dunnii

Streptocarpus galpinii

ACANTHACEAE

Leaves are usually opposite and the inflorescences often have conspicuous bracts amongst the flowers.

Chaetacanthus burchellii

A bushy shrublet up to 300 mm high with fine soft hairs and slender reddish stems. The broad, oval leaves are up to 20 mm long. The inflorescences have maroon bracts amongst the white or pale pink flowers which are 5-lobed and approximately 8 mm wide. Flowering takes place from August to February. Grows in sunny grassland at medium to high altitudes in the southern districts.

Ruellia patula

This dainty plant is up to 200 mm high, is covered with hairs and has ovate leaves about 25 mm long. The flower is generally mauve, but occasionally white. It is about 20 mm wide with a slender tube that divides into 5 lobes with purple stripes. Flowering takes place from October to March. Grows in open woodland, mainly at low to medium altitudes and has been recorded from north to south.

Crossandra greenstockii Crossandra

This charming perennial is up to 300 mm high with soft leaves which are more or less oval and about 100 mm long. The dense inflorescence has numerous pointed, hairy bracts and shimmering flowers, 20–40 mm wide, salmon to deep orange, with yellow in the throat. There are 5 shallow corolla lobes arranged asymmetrically as though there should have been a sixth lobe. From October to December these cheerful flowers provide a welcome splash of colour in the new green grass. Found in wooded or rocky grassland at various altitudes, from north to south.

Blepharis subvolubilis var. subvolubilis

An extremely prickly, ground-hugging perennial up to 300 mm high, with prostrate or semi-erect stems and short rough hairs. The oval leaves are 20–50 mm long with coarse, spine-tipped serrations. The inflorescences have large prickly bracts and blue-mauve flowers, each with a single showy, striped lobe about 20 mm long. Flowering takes place from October to January. Grows in grassland, in the south.

Chaetacanthus burchellii

Ruellia patula

Crossandra greenstockii

Blepharis subvolubilis var. *subvolubilis*

ACANTHACEAE

Ruttya ovata

A somewhat lanky shrub 2–4 m high with broad lanceolate leaves up to 100 mm long. The dense inflorescence is about 50 mm long with numerous long, slender bracts and sepals which give it a shaggy, slightly unkempt appearance. The crowded 2-lipped flowers are white with maroon spots and generally open from January to March. Occurs at various altitudes on forest margins and shaded, rocky outcrops. Recorded from a few localities in the central and southern areas.

Macrorungia longistrobus

This rather rare shrub has been grown successfully in a few private gardens and in the Lowveld Botanic Garden at Nelspruit. It grows 2–3 m high with broadly lanceolate leaves up to 80 mm long. The dense inflorescence has sharp-tipped bracts with transparent margins and 2-lipped yellow-orange flowers about 30 mm long. The upper lip is conspicuous, the lower very small. Flowering takes place from March to May, when the plant is constantly visited by sunbirds. Recorded from only a few localities: near the Abel Erasmus Pass, at Louw's Creek and from the hills in the southern Kruger National Park, near Malelane.

Dicliptera clinopodia

Inconspicuous for most of the year, this perennial has brilliant little flowers which catch the eye in autumn and winter. It grows up to 1 m high and the oval leaves are up to 60 mm long. The dense inflorescence has narrow maroon bracts and 2-lipped purple or magenta flowers 10–15 mm long. Flowering takes place mainly from March to July. Grows on forest margins and the banks of streams at various altitudes over virtually the entire region.

Mackaya bella Forest Bell Bush, Blouklokkiesbos

This shade-loving shrub is an excellent and very popular garden subject. It is 1–3 m high and has glossy, broadly lanceolate leaves up to 100 mm long. The exquisite, pale lilac flowers have 5 curved corolla lobes with faint maroon markings along the veins. Flowering takes place from September to December. Grows in evergreen forests high up in the mountains and recorded from scattered localities from north to south.

Ruttya ovata

Macrorungia longistrobus

Dicliptera clinopodia

Mackaya bella

RUBIACEAE

Commonly called the "gardenia family". Leaves are opposite or whorled, usually with an interpetiolar stipule linking the petioles.

Gardenia amoena Thorny Gardenia, Doringkatjiepiering

A spiny shrub or tree 2–6 m high with glossy obovate leaves about 40 mm long, crowded on short lateral shoots. The fragrant white flowers, 50 mm wide, have spreading lobes which are edged with red below, so that the unopened bud is red. Flowering takes place from November to March. The small round fruits are topped with the persistent calyx. Occurs in a variety of habitats, from rocky outcrops to bushy ravines, mainly at medium to high altitudes.

Gardenia spatulifolia Transvaal Gardenia, Transvaalse Katjiepiering

The hard angular appearance of this rigid tree is softened by the glossy leaves and attractive waxy-white flowers. It is 3–6 m high with obovate, undulate leaves 20–60 mm long which are clustered on short, stubby lateral shoots. The fragrant white flowers, about 80 mm wide, age to yellow and the slender co-rolla tube is up to 100 mm long. Flowering takes place briefly, from September to November. The oval, grey-green fruits are about 60 mm long and have a ribbed, warty surface. Grows in open woodland of low to medium altitudes.

Burchellia bubalina Wild Pomegranate, Wildegranaat

This is one of the few indigenous shrubs that has been widely utilised in horti-culture. With its dark green foliage and bright flowers it is a most rewarding subject and, because of its abundant nectar, it is a great favourite with sun-birds. It grows 2–5 m high and the oval leaves are about 100 mm long. The orange to red tubular flowers are about 20 mm long and are borne in clusters from September to December. The fruits, about 5 mm in diameter and topped with the persistent calyxes, look like miniature pomegranates. Recorded from the central and southern mountains, mainly on forest margins.

Rothmannia globosa September Bells, Klokkieskatjiepiering

Conspicuous in bloom, this is one of the most beautiful forest plants in the region. It is a bushy shrub or small tree 3–5 m high with narrow leaves about 50 mm long. The fragrant ivory, bell-shaped flowers, which have reflexed co-rolla lobes, are borne in profusion in spring and early summer. The round fruit is topped with the persistent calyx. Grows in evergreen forest on the moun-tains, from north to south.

Gardenia amoena

Gardenia spatulifolia

Burchellia bubalina

Rothmannia globosa

RUBIACEAE

Pentanisia prunelloides Wild Verbena, Wildeverbena

This is one of the first plants to grace the spring veld of this region with its pretty flowers. It is a variable, hairy perennial up to 400 mm high which may be single- or multi-stemmed and the variable leaves occur mainly near the base of the plant. The striking inflorescence, about 30 mm in diameter, is dense and almost spherical, with pale to dark blue little flowers. Flowering takes place from August to December. Grows in open rocky grassland at medium to high altitudes.

Bride's Bush is a fitting name for the pavettas: their beautiful inflorescences would be eminently suitable for bridal bouquets. The massed flowers are white and fragrant, with 4–5 small, spreading corolla lobes and protruding style. The leaves have bacterial dots which show up against the light.

Pavetta gracilifolia (=P. breyeri) Small Bride's Bush, Kleinbruidsbos

Around mid-summer the enchanting flowers of this perennial soften the harsh granite boulders of their natural habitat. The plant is either a shrub up to 2 m high, or it may be prostrate, sprawling over rock faces. The hairy lanceolate leaves are about 20 mm long and the rounded inflorescences up to 50 mm wide. Somewhat rare and localised, it has been recorded only from the south, at medium altitudes.

Pavetta edentula Large-leaved Bride's Bush, Grootblaarbruidsbos

This rugged tree is superb in bloom. It grows 2–5 m high with stubby brittle branches and glossy lanceolate leaves up to 200 mm long. The large striking inflorescences are up to 200 mm in diameter and are usually situated just below the terminal leaf clusters. Flowering takes place from October to January. Grows on the southern mountains and foothills: there is a spectacular colony at the foot of the pass between Nelspruit and Barberton.

Pavetta schumanniana Poison Bride's Bush, Gifbruidsbos

This beautiful plant is unpopular with farmers as it causes "gousiekte" in domestic animals. It grows 2–4 m high and has velvety leaves up to 150 mm long. The magnificent inflorescences, which are round or oblong, are held just below the leaf clusters. Flowering takes place from October to January. Grows in open woodland and on rocky outcrops of various altitudes, over the entire region.

Pentanisia prunelloides

Pavetta gracilifolia (=P. breyeri)

Pavetta edentula

Pavetta schumanniana

CUCURBITACEAE

Cucumis anguria var. *longipes* Wild Cucumber, Wildekomkommer

This rough scrambler is covered with short hairs and has slender stems and tendrils. The 3–5-lobed leaves vary in shape and are 30–80 mm long, with serrated margins. The cream, funnel-shaped flowers are 20–30 mm wide and open during the summer months. The yellow fruits, initially marked with light and dark green stripes, have soft curved spines and are about 40 mm long. Occurs in low to medium altitude scrub and open grassland.

Cucumis metuliferus Jelly Melon, Horned Cucumber, Rooikomkommer

This rough, hairy climber has stems several metres long and slender tendrils. The 3–5-lobed leaves are approximately heart-shaped and about 60 mm long, with serrated margins. The yellow, funnel-shaped flowers are about 15 mm wide, opening from December to March. The oblong fruits, 60–120 mm long, are marbled green, ripening to bright orange and have hard, sharp spines. The flesh is often sweet and is eaten raw or cooked. Occurs in bush or grassland at various altitudes.

Lagenaria mascarena Wildekalbas

Trees and undergrowth festooned with the large, decorative fruits of this vigorous climber, make an arresting display. It has slender tendrils which are generally forked and the leaves coarsely irregularly 5-lobed, with irregular teeth on the margins. The white, saucer-shaped flowers are about 80 mm wide and open from February to April. The hard, heavy fruits are roughly oblong to round, almost 100 mm long, and are dark green with transverse yellow-green markings. Found in riverine bush at low altitudes.

Momordica foetida

A slender climber with tendrils and triangularly heart-shaped leaves about 80 mm long which have an unpleasant odour when crushed. The crinkly, pale apricot flowers, about 30 mm wide, have black and orange markings in the throat. Flowering takes place from December to February. The round yellow fruit has soft curved spines and splits open into 3 sections, revealing a number of seeds in sticky red flesh. Despite their strange odour the leaves are cooked and eaten as a form of spinach. Occurs in bushy places and along stream banks at medium to high altitudes.

Cucumis anguria var. *longipes*

Cucumis metuliferus

Lagenaria mascarena

Momordica foetida

LOBELIACEAE

Lobelia decipiens Wild Lobelia, Wildelobelia

Although it can reach 400 mm in height, this dainty perennial is generally much smaller. It has narrow leaves about 10 mm long and the 2-lipped flowers are up to 20 mm long. The upper, 2-lobed lip is purple and the lower, 3-lobed, is pale blue with yellow at the base. Flowering takes place during the summer months, only after rain has fallen. Found mainly at medium to high altitudes, in damp grassland or in shallow rock depressions.

ASTERACEAE (=COMPOSITAE)

This is the large and well-known daisy family. A "daisy" is in fact not a flower but an inflorescence, consisting of massed tiny flowers called florets, borne on a common base and surrounded and supported by a calyx-like involucre of bracts e.g. *Helichrysum.* In certain genera the florets comprise disc-florets massed in the centre and surrounded by a ring of ray-florets, each of which has a showy ribbon-like "petal" e.g. *Gerbera.*

Mikania cordata

This vigorous scrambler has heart-shaped leaves about 60 mm long with irregularly toothed margins. The inflorescence is a lax spray of fragrant, tiny white flower heads, each one narrow, cylindrical and about 10 mm long. Flowering takes place from July to September. Grows at various altitudes in riverine bush and on forest margins.

Vernonia stipulacea (= V. ampla)

This showy, bushy shrub is a distinctive feature of this region's autumn and early winter landscape. It is 2–4 m high, with velvety stems and leaves. The oval leaves are up to 150 mm long with serrated, undulate margins. The large, branched inflorescences are pale mauve, soon fading to white. The densely massed, tiny tubular flower heads are about 10 mm long. Flowering takes place from April to June. Found mainly at medium to high altitudes in open or riverine woodland and often on road verges.

Vernonia sutherlandii

The brilliant colour of these inflorescences immediately catches the eye. It is an erect perennial up to 600 mm high with broadly lanceolate, velvety leaves 40–60 mm long, which have coarsely serrated margins. The inflorescence is branched, with magenta or royal purple heads which are about 10 mm long. The involucral bracts are narrow, pointed and velvety. Flowering takes place from August to November. Grows in open, rocky grassland or woodland of medium to high altitudes in the central and southern districts.

Lobelia decipiens

Mikania cordata

Vernonia stipulacea (=V. ampla)

Vernonia sutherlandii

ASTERACEAE

Everlasting is a good name for the papery helichrysums which are so popular for posies, dried flower arrangements, corsages etc. The Afrikaans name is equally appropriate, implying a life of 7 years.

Helichrysum acutatum Everlasting, Sewejaartjie

The sparkling yellow flowers of this perennial are a perfect foil for the soft silver leaves. It is multi-stemmed and up to 600 mm high with grey velvety stems and narrow leaves which are up to 150 mm long. The branched inflorescence is 50–60 mm wide, with numerous tiny yellow flower heads. Flowering takes place from August to November. It flowers best in burnt veld and has been recorded at medium to high altitudes in the central and southern regions.

Helichrysum adenocarpum subsp. *adenocarpum* Red Everlasting, Rooisewejaartjie

This is one of the most colourful everlastings in the region. It has a basal rosette of silver, woolly, oval leaves that are about 40 mm long, with shorter, overlapping leaves along the procumbent stems. The flower heads, about 25 mm wide, are quite magnificent: golden-yellow florets surrounded by shiny pink and red involucral bracts. Flowering takes place from February to May. Grows in grassland high up in the mountains and recorded from north to south.

Helichrysum appendiculatum Everlasting, Sheep's Ears, Sewejaartjie, Skaapoorbossie

This woolly perennial is erect and up to 600 mm high, with slender lanceolate leaves about 80 mm long. The inflorescence is a branched cluster of flower heads which are about 15 mm wide and the numerous involucral bracts, longer than the yellow florets, are off-white to rose-pink or red. Flowering usually takes place from December to February. Grows in high altitude vleis in the central and southern regions.

Helichrysum chionosphaerum Everlasting, Sewejaartjie

This rock-hugging little perennial sprawls out of rock crevices and is up to 100 mm high with procumbent woody stems. The narrow dark green leaves are about 60 mm long and white-felted below. The charming little "cupcake" flower heads are about 15 mm wide. The involucral bracts are white or cream, spreading open wide as the head opens and the dome of yellow florets is slightly raised. Flowering takes place from August to December. It forms dense mats in open, rocky grassland on the central and southern mountains.

Helichrysum acutatum

Helichrysum adenocarpum subsp. *adenocarpum*

Helichrysum appendiculatum

Helichrysum chionosphaerum

ASTERACEAE

Helichrysum cooperi Yellow Everlasting, Geelsewejaartjie

This handsome, robust perennial is aromatic, slightly sticky and covered with fine soft hairs. It is erect and up to 1 m high with broadly lanceolate or oval leaves up to 90 mm long. The glowing, golden-yellow flower heads are about 20 mm wide with the involucral bracts longer than the florets. Flowering takes place from January to March. Grows in vleis along the escarpment.

Helichrysum kraussii Everlasting, Sewejaartjie

A bushy shrub up to 1 m high with numerous narrow leaves up to 10 mm long which are grey-green above and pale grey below, with inrolled margins. The inflorescence is branched, 20–40 mm wide, with numerous tiny, almost cylindrical heads which are dull yellow. Flowering takes place from July to September. Common in rocky, scrubby grassland at medium to high altitudes.

Helichrysum mimetes Curry Everlasting, Kerriesewejaartjie

This aromatic perennial has a strong curry smell which is evident even in herbarium specimens that are over 50 years old. It is a straggly shrublet 200–500 mm high, with woolly stems and leaves. The grey leaves are more or less oval and about 25 mm long. The inflorescence is a branched but compact cluster, 25–30 mm wide, of small, lemon-coloured flower heads, the florets being slightly longer than the oyster-coloured involucral bracts. Flowering takes place from May to August. Grows in rocky places at high altitudes.

Helichrysum reflexum White Everlasting, Witsewejaartjie

Found in colonies along the escarpment, this bushy shrublet blends beautifully with the white-lichened grey rocks. It is woolly and 200–500 mm high, with narrowly linear leaves up to 100 mm long, with inrolled margins. The flower heads are 20–25 mm wide with shiny buff-pink involucral bracts which are white on the inside and are longer than the yellow florets. Flowering takes place from late summer into early autumn. Recorded from the central and southern mountains.

Helichrysum cooperi

Helichrysum kraussii

Helichrysum mimetes

Helichrysum reflexum

ASTERACEAE

Helichrysum sp.aff. *H. setosum* Yellow Everlasting, Geelsewejaartjie

An erect, sparsely branched shrub up to 1,5 m high, inclined to become some-what straggly. It has lanceolate leaves up to 80 mm long covered wtih rough hairs. The beautiful flower heads are up to 25 mm wide, with glossy yellow involucral bracts which are longer than the minute yellow florets. These open from March to August. Grows on rocky outcrops and in bushy places on the central and southern mountains and foothills.

Stoebe vulgaris Zig-zag Bush, Slangbos, Asbos

This straggly, tangled, ericoid shrub is a distinctive feature of rocky places and cliff edges on the escarpment. It is 1–2 m high with grey stems and clusters of minute grey leaves, 2–3 mm long. The inflorescence is a small cluster of tiny, single-flowered heads. The plant is often gall-infested, resulting in little pear-shaped blobs of white "cotton wool" which are sometimes mistaken for the inflorescences. Flowering takes place from May to August. Recorded from the central and southern mountains.

Athrixia phylicoides Bush Tea, Bostee

An infusion of this bush is used as tea. It grows up to 1 m high with neat lan-ceolate leaves 20–30 mm long which are grey-green above and white-felted below. The pretty daisies are about 15 mm wide, with mauve to purple ray-florets and orange disc-florets. The cone-shaped involucre is 10 mm long and has tiny, neatly arranged, purple-tipped bracts. Flowering takes place from June to November. Grows in dappled shade in rocky, wooded grassland of medium to high altitudes.

Callilepis laureola Ox-eye Daisy, Wildemargriet

An erect, multi-stemmed perennial with a large woody rootstock, ribbed hairy stems and lanceolate leaves about 60 mm long. The attractive daisies are 50–60 mm wide, with ivory ray-florets and black disc-florets. Flowering takes place from September to December. Despite the fact that the rootstock is very poisonous, and can be fatal, a decoction of it is used medicinally. Grows in sunny grassland at various altitudes in the south.

Helichrysum sp. aff. *H. setosum*

Stoebe vulgaris

Athrixia phylicoides

Callilepis laureola

ASTERACEAE

Athanasia acerosa

In late summer and autumn this handsome perennial is a conspicuous component of the escarpment scenery. It is a robust, multi-stemmed shrub which grows up to 1 m high and has densely crowded narrow leaves which are about 30 mm long with 3–7 slender lobes. The striking inflorescences have massed, tiny, bright yellow flower heads and flowering takes place from February to June. Relatively common in grassland on the central and southern escarpment and foothills.

Brachymeris bolusii

Another autumn-flowering shrub, it is colourful amongst the rocks of the escarpment. It is bushy and up to 1 m high with narrowly linear leaves 10–30 mm long. The somewhat flat-topped inflorescences have yellow flower heads 5–7 mm wide, with the involucral bracts slightly shorter than the minute crowded florets. Flowering takes place from May to August. Recorded from a few scattered localities along the escarpment.

Senecio tamoides Canary Creeper, Goue Reën

This lovely senecio is an extremely popular garden plant. It is a soft, semi-succulent scrambler and has broadly triangular leaves, about 70 mm long, with a few irregular, toothed lobes. The flower heads, borne in loose, rounded sprays, are 15–20 mm wide, with yellow ray- and disc-florets. Flowering is irregular, but occurs mainly during autumn and winter. Grows in forest in scattered localities along the escarpment.

Senecio pleistocephalus

A robust, semi-succulent scrambler with broadly oval leaves that are about 70 mm long with irregularly serrated margins. The slightly domed inflorescences are loosely branched, with massed, tiny, bright yellow flower heads. It is most attractive in full bloom but the flowers soon fade to brown. Flowering takes place from April to July. Recorded from north to south, in low to medium altitude woodland.

Athanasia acerosa

Brachymeris bolusii

Senecio tamoides

Senecio pleistocephalus

ASTERACEAE

Osteospermum jucundum Bergbietou, Bloubietou

A spreading, sprawling plant with lanceolate to oval leaves about 60 mm long. The margins occasionally have a few irregular blunt teeth. The daisy is exquisite: the ray-florets are rich mauve or magenta above and copper below, while the disc-florets, tipped with black, open to yellow. The head is up to 50 mm wide and flowering takes place from August to March. This lovely plant graces rocky grassland on the central and southern escarpment and foothills.

Haplocarpha scaposa Tontelbossie, Bietou

This perennial grows 250–300 mm high with a basal rosette of undulate oval leaves about 120 mm long which are densely white-felted below. The bright sunny daisy, usually 40–50 mm wide, has yellow ray- and disc-florets and the narrow, felted involucral bracts have transparent margins. Flowering takes place from August to December. Occurs in medium to high altitude grassland in the central and southern districts.

Gazania krebsiana subsp. *serrulata* Gazania, Botterblom, Kleingousblommetjie

This ground-hugging perennial is like a burst of brilliant sunshine in the veld. It grows up to 100 mm high with tufts of basal leaves which are about 50 mm long and dark green above, grey-felted below. The striking daisy is about 50 mm wide with bright yellow ray- and disc-florets. Occasional plants have white flower heads. Flowering takes place from July to September. Grows in open grassland on the central and southern escarpment and foothills.

Dicoma zeyheri Doll's Protea, Jakkalsbos

While the inflorescence of this perennial may well bear a superficial resemblance to a small protea it is, however, not remotely related to that family. It is a prickly shrublet 200–300 mm high with lanceolate to oval leaves which are up to 120 mm long, white-felted below. The flower heads are 40–50 mm wide with satiny but hard, mauve-green involucral bracts which have sharp tips and are longer than the florets. Flowering takes place from December to May. Grows in open rocky grassland on the central and southern escarpment and foothills.

Osteospermum jucundum

Haplocarpha scaposa

Gazania krebsiana subsp. *serrulata*

Dicoma zeyheri

ASTERACEAE

Berkheya latifolia Disseldoring

An erect, bristly perennial up to 600 mm high which has ovate to oblong leaves with spiny margins. The beautiful sunny daisy is about 60 mm wide with clear yellow ray- and disc-florets. The narrow involucral bracts are very bristly. Flowering takes place from October to April. Found in marshes and along the banks of streams of the southern mountains.

Berkheya zeyheri subsp. *rehmannii*

One of the finest daisies in the region, it positively sparkles in the spring and early summer veld. It is 600–900 mm high and has narrow lanceolate leaves about 80 mm long. They are smooth, dark green above, white-felted below, with prickly margins. The superb daisy, 60–90 mm wide, has yellow ray- and disc-florets. The involucral bracts are long and narrow with long bristles. Flowering takes place from October to January. Found in open grassland at various altitudes in the central and southern districts.

Gerbera kraussii

This sturdy, downy perennial is 150–300 mm high with a few oval to ovate basal leaves about 80 mm long and covered with thick white felt on the lower surface. The pretty, white or pink daisies are 50–60 mm wide, with the black-tipped disc-florets opening to the same colour as the rays. Flowering takes place from August to November. Recorded from a few scattered localities in the south, in the medium to high altitude grassland.

Gerbera jamesonii Barberton Daisy, Barbertonse Madeliefie

The world-famous and well-loved Barberton Daisy is a parent plant of the colourful hybrids grown in gardens, parks, pots and hothouses all over the world. It is up to 400 mm high with a basal rosette of leaves 200–300 mm long which are irregularly lobed and toothed. The charming daisy, about 80 mm wide, has deep orange to rich red rays and yellow to orange disc-florets. Some variants in pale colours have been recorded, with salmon or yellow rays. Flowering takes place from August to December. Grows in light shade on medium altitude rocky outcrops and is more common in the south than in the north.

Berkheya latifolia

Berkheya zeyheri subsp. *rehmannii*

Gerbera kraussii

Gerbera jamesonii

GLOSSARY

alternate: arranged alternately, one above the other (fig. 1)

anther: upper, pollen-bearing portion of stamen (fig. 6)

axil: angle between stem and leaf stalk (fig. 2)

axillary: situated in the axil

bipinnate: used of a pinnate leaf of which the primary leaflets are themselves pinnately divided (fig. 4)

bulb: underground storage and reproductive organ composed of succulent leaf bases or scales

bract: modified leaf for example at the base of flower or flower stalk

calyx: outer series of floral envelope, consisting of sepals which are usually green (fig. 6)

compound: consisting of several similar parts

corm: underground storage or reproductive organ which is a modified stem

corolla: inner series of floral envelope, usually visually attractive, consisting of petals which may be united or separate (fig. 6)

corona: 5-lobed "crown" of appendages between the stamens and corolla, as in Asclepiadaceae (fig. 9)

crisped: with minute undulations

deciduous: shedding leaves at a particular season

dentate: toothed (fig. 5)

digitate: with leaflets radiating from a central point like the spread fingers of a hand (fig. 4)

disc-floret: tubular floret in central portion of flower head as in Asteraceae (fig. 11)

entire: smooth and even, without teeth (fig. 5)

epiphyte: plant growing on another plant, but not as a parasite

evergreen: bearing leaves throughout the year

family: taxonomic rank containing related genera

filament: anther-bearing stalk of stamen (fig. 6)

floral envelope: calyx-and-corolla, or perianth

floret: small flower, portion of a flower head

gall: abnormal growth caused by disease or attack by pest

genus: taxonomic rank containing related species

herb: plant with no persistent woody parts

herbarium: a scientific collection of preserved or dried plant specimens

inflorescence: flowering shoot bearing more than one flower

involucral bracts: one or more series of bracts supporting a flower head (fig. 11)

keel: lower, keel-shaped petal of certain flowers e.g. Papilionoideae and Polygalaceae (fig. 8)

keeled: shaped like the keel of a boat

lanceolate: lance-shaped, tapering towards the apex (fig. 3)

latex: milky fluid produced by certain plants

leaflet: one portion of a compound leaf

linear: long and narrow, the margins almost parallel (fig. 3)

lip: one of the lobes of a 2-lipped corolla (fig. 10) or the dissimilar, distinctive petal in Orchidaceae (fig. 7)

lobe: portion or division of a leaf, calyx or petal, too large to be defined as a tooth

node: point on a stem where a leaf or leaves emerge (fig. 2)

oblanceolate: reverse lanceolate, tapering towards the base (fig. 3)

oblong: longer than broad, with margins almost parallel (fig. 3)

obovate: reverse egg-shape, broadest in top half (fig. 3)

Fig. 1 Arrangement of leaves

alternate   opposite   whorled

Fig. 2 A typical leaf

axil, apex, margin, vein, midrib, blade, base, petiole, axillary bud, stipule, stem, node

Fig. 3 Leaf shapes

linear   oblong   lanceolate   oblanceolate   ovate   obovate   oval

Fig. 4 Leaf types

simple   rachis   leaflet   pinnate   bipinnate   tripinnate   rachis   digitately compound   trifoliate   palmately lobed (simpel)

Fig. 5 Leaf margins

entire   serrated   dentate   undulate

Fig. 6 Typical flower

stigma, style, anther, filament, stamen (male organ), pistil (female organ), ovary, ovule, petal, sepal

Fig. 7 Orchidaceae

sepal, lip, petal, hooded dorsal sepal, spur, sepal

Fig. 10 Lamiaceae

upper lip, corolla tube, lower lip

Fig. 8 Polygalaceae

crest, keel, wing

Fig. 9 Asclepiadaceae

corona lobes, corolla lobes

Fig. 11 Asteraceae

ray-floret, disc-floret, involucral bract

207

opposite: 2 at a node, on opposite sides of stem (fig. 1)

oval: broadest in the centre, tapering towards base and apex (fig. 3)

ovary: lowest portion of pistil which, after fertilisation, becomes the fruit (fig. 6)

ovate: egg-shaped, broadest in lower half (fig. 3)

ovule: incipient seed (fig. 6)

palmate: with lobes arranged like spread-out hand (fig. 4)

parasitic: growing on another plant and drawing nourishment from it

peduncle: stalk of inflorescence

perianth: used here to denote floral envelope of those plants where the calyx and corolla cannot be differentiated e.g. Liliaceae

persistent: remaining on the plant

petal: corolla lobe or segment, usually coloured, often conspicuous (fig. 6)

petiole: stalk of a leaf (fig. 2)

pinnate: with leaflets arranged in 2 opposite ranks (fig. 4)

pistil: female unit of flower, consisting of stigma, style, ovary (fig. 6)

procumbent: lying on the ground for most of its length

pseudobulb: swollen, bulb-like internode, as in some orchids

rachis: common stalk to which leaflets are attached (fig. 4)

ray-floret: petal-like floret on margin of flower head as in Asteraceae (fig. 11)

reflexed: turned back, often abruptly

reticulated: lattice-like

rhizome: elongated underground stem, sometimes fleshy, usually horizontal, which produces roots and shoots

sepal: calyx lobe or segment, usually green (fig. 6)

serrated: saw-toothed, as of a margin (fig. 5)

sessile: having no stalk

spadix: fleshy spike of small flowers, enclosed in spathe

spathe: large bract which encloses spadix, as in Araceae

spikelet: unit of inflorescence, as in Cyperaceae

species: generally the smallest unit of classification, it may be sub-divided into subspecies and/or varieties

spur: hollow, tubular extension of petal or sepal, sometimes containing nectar, as in Orchidaceae (fig. 7) or *Impatiens*

stamen: male unit of flower, consisting of filament and anther (fig. 6)

stigma: that part of pistil which receives the pollen (fig. 6)

stipule: basal, leaf-like appendage of petiole, usually occurring in pairs (fig. 2)

style: narrow portion of pistil which bears stigma (fig. 6)

taxonomy: science of classification of living organisms

terminal: situated at the apex

tepal: perianth segment or lobe

trifoliate: having 3 leaflets (fig. 4)

tuber: underground, modifed root or stem, acting as storage organ and capable of vegetative reproduction

undulate: wavy, as of a leaf margin (fig. 5)

whorl: arrangement of 3 of more leaves at the same level (fig. 1)

ERRATA

PHOTOGRAPHIC CREDITS/FOTOGRAFIESE ERKENNINGS

Jo Onderstall Front cover/voorblad: *Gerbera jamesonii*. Back cover/agterblad: *Sterculia murex*. Bill Fraser: *Gerbera* sp. 22, 23

INDEX TO BOTANICAL NAMES/INDEKS TOT BOTANIESE NAME

ACANTHACEAE, 183
Becium obovatum (E. Mey. ex Benth.) N.E. Br. var. galpinii (Guerke) N.E. Br., 173
Berkheya latifolia Wood & Evans, 205
Berkheya zeyheri (Sond. & Harv.) Oliv. & Hiern subsp. rehmannii (Thell.) Roessl., 205
BIGNONIACEAE, 179
Blepharis subvolubilis C.B. Cl. var. subvolubilis, 183
Bolusanthus speciosus (H.Bol.) Harms, 109
Boophane disticha Herb., 53
Brachymeris bolusii Hutch., 201
*Brachystelma gracile E.A. Bruce, 163
Brunsvigia natalensis Bak., 55
Brunsvigia radulosa Herb., 55
BURSERACEAE, 121
CAESALPINIOIDEAE, 105
*Calanthe natalensis (Reichb.f.) Reichb.f., 73
*Calanthe sylvatica (Thou.) Lindl., 73
Calodendrum capense (L.f.) Thunb., 119
Canavalia virosa (Roxb.) Wight & Arn., 117
Cyanotis speciosa (L.f.) Hassk., 37
◆Sesbania punicea (Cav.) Benth., 111
THYMELAEACEAE, 139

INDEX TO COMMON NAMES/INDEKS TOT VOLKSNAME

*Afrikaanse Suikerbos, 87
*Reuseaasblom, 163
Rooiblaarrotsvy, 81
Usnea sp. 13

Index to Botanical Names

Protected species are marked with an asterisk *
Introduced species are marked ♦

213

TYPHACEAE, 31

UMBELLIFERAE, 145

Vellozia retinervis Bak., 57
VELLOZIACEAE, 57
VERBENACEAE, 167
Vernonia ampla O. Hoffm., 193
Vernonia stipulacea Klatt, 193
Vernonia sutherlandii Harv., 193

* Watsonia transvaalensis Bak., 65
* Watsonia watsonioides (Bak.) Oberm., 65

Xerophyta retinervis Bak., 57
Xysmalobium acerateoides (Schltr.)
    N.E. Br., 155
Xysmalobium undulatum (L.) Ait.f., 155

ZAMIACEAE, 29
* Zantedeschia aethiopica (L.) Spreng., 35
* Zantedeschia rehmannii Engl., 35
ZINGIBERACEAE, 67

Index to Common Names

Protected species are marked with an asterisk *   Introduced species are marked ◆

216

Photographic credits

Lynette Davidson   *Buttonia superba* 177.

Peter Durrant   *Encephalartos laevifolius* 29.

Steve Fourie   *Encephalartos transvenosus* 29; *Brunsvigia radulosa* 55; *Erica cerinthoides* var. *cerinthoides* (red form) 147.

Bill Fraser   *Gerbera* sp. Cover; *Zantedeschia aethiopica* 35; *Zantedeschia rehmannii* 35; *Haemanthus hirsutus* 53; *Schizostylis coccinea* 61; *Protea roupelliae* subsp. *roupelliae* 89; *Calodendrum capense* 119; *Hypericum revolutum* 135; *Erica cerinthoides* var. *cerinthoides* (pink form) 147; *Clerodendrum triphyllum* 167; *Streptocarpus cyaneus* 181; *Rothmannia globosa* 187; *Helichrysum adenocarpum* 195.

Johan Kluge   *Kniphofia linearifolia* 41; *Cynorkis kassneriana* 67; *Brachycorythis pleistophylla* 69; *Disa nervosa* 71; *Cyrtorchis arcuata* 79; *Impatiens sylvicola* 129; *Plectranthus fruticosus* 171; *Cycnium racemosum* 175.

I. C. Nel   *Littonia modesta* 39; *Gladiolus dalenii* 63; *Watsonia watsonioides* 65; *Satyrium trinerve* 69; *Disa chrysostachya* 71; *Disa stachyoides* 71; *Herschelia baurii* 71; *Eulophia foliosa* 75; *Eulophia speciosa* 77; *Pearsonia aristata* 109; *Erica drakensbergensis* 147; *Erica woodii* 147; *Pachycarpus campanulatus* 157; *Pachycarpus transvaalensis* 157; *Striga elegans* 175; *Streptocarpus dunnii* 181; *Lobelia decipiens* 193.

Bill Onderstall   *Siphonochilus aethiopicus* 67; *Acampe praemorsa* 79; *Dichrostachys cinerea* subsp. *nyassana* 103; *Oncoba spinosa* 135.

PROTECTED PLANTS OF THE TRANSVAAL
Schedule 7 of Ordinance 17 of 1967 and A.N. 1714 dd. 1.10.1975

Common names	Scientific names
All species of tree moss	Genera *Porothamnium, Pilotrichella* and *Papillaria*
all species of ferns other than the bracken fern	Division Pteridophyta, except *Pteridium aquilinum*
all species of yellowwood	Genus *Podocarpus*
all species of wild cypress	Genus *Widdringtonia*
borassus palm	*Borassus flabellifer*
all species of arum lilies	Genus *Zantedeschia*
all species of Agapanthus except improved plants	Genus *Agapanthus*
all species of aloes except all species not occurring in the Transvaal and the following species: *A. aculeata, A. ammophila, A. barbertoniae, A. castanea, A. davyana, A. globuligemma, A. grandidentata, A. lutescens, A. marlothii, A. mutans, A. parvibracteata, A. transvaalensis, A. wickensii*	Genus *Aloe*
all species of Chortolirion	Genus *Chortolirion*
all species of Dracaena	Genus *Dracaena*
all species of pineapple flowers	Genus *Eucomis*
all species of Galtonia	Genus *Galtonia*
all species of Gasteria	Genus *Gasteria*
all species of flame lilies	Genus *Gloriosa*
all species of Haworthia	Genus *Haworthia*
all species of red-hot-pokers	Genus *Kniphofia*
all species of Christmas bells	Genus *Littonia*
blue squill	*Scilla natalensis*
ground lily	*Ammocharis coranica*
fire lily	*Anoiganthus breviflorus*
pink brunsvigia	*Brunsvigia radulosa*
all species of Clivia	Genus *Clivia*
all species of Crinum	Genus *Crinum*
all species of fire lilies	Genus *Cyrtanthus*
all species of paintbrush	Genus *Haemanthus* including *Scadoxus*
all species of Nerine	Genus *Nerine*
all species of elephant's foot	Genus *Dioscorea*
all species of Babiana	Genus *Babiana*
wild montbretia	*Crocosmia paniculata*
all species of harebells	Genus *Dierama*
all species of wild iris	Genus *Dietes*
all species of gladiolus except improved plants	Genus *Gladiolus*
all species of Lapeirousia	Genus *Lapeirousia*
river lily	*Schizostylis coccinea*

all species of Watsonia except improved plants	Genus *Watsonia*
wild banana	*Ensete ventricosum*
Transvaal strelitzia	*Strelitzia caudata*
wild ginger	*Siphonochilus aethiopicus* and *Burmannia madagascariensis*
all species of orchids	Family ORCHIDACEAE
pincushion	*Leucospermum gerrardii*
all species of Protea	Genus *Protea*
stone plant	*Frithia pulchra*
all species of stone plants	Genus *Lithops*
all species of water lilies	Genus *Nymphaea* and *Brassenia schreberi*
wonder plant	*Tinospora fragosum*
black stinkwood	*Ocotea bullata*
stinkwood	*Ocotea kenyensis*
transvaal teak (kiaat)	*Pterocarpus angolensis*
the following species of Euphorbia	Genus *Euphorbia*
E. barnardii, E. grandialata, E. groenewaldii, E. knobelii, E. perangusta, E. restricta, E. rowlandii, E. tortirama, E. waterbergensis	
tambootie	*Spirostachys africana*
baobab	*Adansonia digitata*
all species of Begonia	Genus *Begonia*
all species of cabbage tree	Genus *Cussonia*
heath	*Erica oatesii*
red hairy heath	*Erica cerinthoides*
heath	*Erica alopecurus*
big leaf (wild tobacco)	*Anthocleista grandiflora*
impala lily	*Adenium multiflorum*
impala lily	*Adenium oleifolium*
impala lily	*Adenium swazicum*
kudu lily	*Pachypodium saundersii*
all species of Brachystelma	Genus *Brachystelma*
all species of Caralluma	Genus *Caralluma*
all species of Ceropegia	Genus *Ceropegia*
all species of Tavaresia	Genus *Tavaresia*
all species of Duvalia	Genus *Duvalia*
all species of Huernia and Huerniopsis	Genera *Huernia* and *Huerniopsis*
all species of Riocreuxia	Genus *Riocreuxia*
all species of Stapelia	Genus *Stapelia*
all species of Stultitia	Genus *Stultitia*
all species of cape primula	Genus *Streptocarpus*
barberton daisy except improved plants	*Gerbera jamesonii*

SPECIALLY PROTECTED PLANTS
Schedule 7A of Ordinance 17 of 1967

all species of cycads	Genus *Encephalartos*

THREATENED PLANTS OF THE TRANSVAAL
Hall et. al. 1981

Endangered species

Family	Scientific name	Common name
Zamiaceae	*Encephalartos cupidus*	
	Encephalartos inopinus	Lydenburg Cycad
	Encephalartos laevifolius	Kaapsche Hoop Cycad
Orchidaceae	*Nervilia purpurata*	
Euphorbiaceae	*Euphorbia barnardii*	
	Euphorbia perangusta	

Vulnerable species

Family	Scientific name	Common name
Zamiaceae	*Encephalartos eugene-maraisii*	Waterberg Cycad
	Encephalartos heenanii	Woolly Cycad
	Encephalartos humilis	
	Encephalartos ngoyanus	
	Encephalartos paucidentatus	Barberton Cycad
Liliaceae	*Aloe albida*	White Grass Aloe
	Aloe monotropa	
Iridaceae	*Gladiolus pretoriensis*	
Proteaceae	*Protea curvata*	Barberton Lowveld Protea
Crassulaceae	*Kalanchoe crundallii*	
Euphorbiaceae	*Euphorbia groenewaldii*	
	Euphorbia knobelii	
	Euphorbia rowlandii	
	Euphorbia tortirama	
Canellaceae	*Warburgia salutaris*	Pepper-bark Tree
Asclepiadaceae	*Orbea maculata*	
	Stapelia clavicorona	
	Huernia nouhuysii	

BIBLIOGRAPHY AND RECOMMENDED READING

ACOCKS, J. P. H., 1975. *Veld Types of South Africa. Memoirs of the Botanical Survey of South Africa* 40. 2nd edition. Dept. of Agricultural Technical Services, Pretoria.

BAKER, H. A. and OLIVER, E. G. H., 1967. *Ericas in Southern Africa.* Purnell, Cape Town.

BALL, J. S., 1978. *Southern African epiphytic orchids.* Conservation Press, Johannesburg.

BUITENDAG, E., 1972. *Plantegroei van die Laeveld.* Botany Honours Seminar, University of Pretoria, Pretoria.

CARR, J. D., 1976. *The South African Acacias.* Conservation Press, Johannesburg.

CODD, L. E. W. 1968. *The South African species of Kniphofia. Bothalia* 9 parts 3 and 4. Dept. of Agricultural Technical Services, Pretoria.

CODD, L. E. W., 1975. *Plectranthus (Labiatae) and allied genera in Southern Africa. Bothalia* 11 part 4. Dept. of Agricultural Technical Services, Pretoria.

COMPTON, R. H., 1976. *The flora of Swaziland. Journal of S.A. Botany* suppl. 11. Trustees of the National Botanic Gardens of S.A., Kirstenbosch.

DE WINTER, B., VAHRMEIJER, J. and VON BREITENBACH, F., 1978. *The National List of Trees.* Van Schaik, Pretoria.

DYER, R. A., 1980. *Asclepiadaceae (Brachystelma, Ceropegia, Riocreuxia). Flora of Southern Africa* 27 part 4. Dept. of Agricultural Technical Services, Pretoria.

DYER, R. A., 1965. *The cycads of Southern Africa. Bothalia* 8 part 4. Dept. of Agricultural Technical Services, Pretoria.

DYER, R. A., 1976. *The genera of South African flowering plants*, 1 and 2. *Flora of Southern Africa.* Dept. of Agricultural Technical Services, Pretoria.

FOX, F. W. and NORWOOD YOUNG, M. E., 1982. *Food from the veld.* Delta Books, Johannesburg.

GIDDY, C., 1974. *Cycads of South Africa.* Purnell, Cape Town.

HALL, A. V., DE WINTER, M. and B., VAN OOSTERHOUT, S. A. M., 1981. *Threatened plants of Southern Africa.* S.A. National Scientific Programmes report no. 45. C.S.I.R., Pretoria.

HARRISON, E. R., 1972. *Epiphytic orchids of Southern Africa.* Natal Branch of the Wildlife Protection and Conservation Society of S.A.

HENDERSON, M. and ANDERSON, J. G., 1966. *Common weeds in South Africa. Memoirs of the Botanical Survey of S.A.* 37. Dept. of Agricultural Technical Services, Pretoria.

HENNESSY, E. F., 1972. *South African Erythrinas.* Natal Branch of the Wildlife Protection and Conservation Society of S.A., Durban.

HILLIARD, O., 1977. *Compositae in Natal.* University of Natal Press, Durban and Pietermaritzburg.

HILLIARD, O. and BURTT, B. L., 1971. *Streptocarpus.* An African plant study. University of Natal Press, Pietermaritzburg.

JEPPE, B., 1969. *South African Aloes.* Purnell, Cape Town.

LETTY, C., 1973. *The genus Zantedeschia. Bothalia* 11 no. 1 and 2. Dept. of Agricultural Technical Services, Pretoria.

LETTY, C., 1962. *Wild flowers of the Transvaal.* Dept. of Agriculture, Pretoria.

LEWIS, G. J., OBERMEYER, A. A. and BARNARD, T. T., 1972. *Gladiolus — a revision of the South African species. Journal of S.A. Botany* suppl. 10. Purnell, Cape Town.

PALGRAVE, K. C., 1977. *Trees of Southern Africa.* C. Struik, Cape Town.

PALMER, E. and PITMAN, N., 1972 and 1973. *Trees of Southern Africa* 1, 2 and 3. A. A. Balkema, Cape Town.

REYNOLDS, G. W., 1970. *The Aloes of Southern Africa.* 2nd edition. A. A. Balkema, Cape Town.

ROSS, J. H., 1979. *A conspectus of the African Acacia species. Memoirs of the Botanical Survey of S.A.* 44. Dept. of Agricultural Technical Services, Pretoria.

ROURKE, J. P., 1980. *The Proteas of Southern Africa.* Purnell, Cape Town.

SCHELPE, E. A. C. L. E., 1966. *An introduction to the South African Orchids.* Purnell, Cape Town.

SMITH, C. A., 1966. *Common names of South African plants. Memoirs of the Botanical Survey of S.A.* 35. Dept. of Agricultural Technical Services, Pretoria.

STEWART, J. and HENNESSY, E. F., 1981. *Orchids of Africa.* Macmillan, Johannesburg.

STEWART, J., LINDER, H. P., SCHELPE, E. A. and HALL, A. V., 1982. *Wild Orchids of Southern Africa.* Macmillan, Johannesburg.

TINLEY, K. L., (no date). *The Kruger National Park.* An ecological inventory prepared for the Wildlife Society, special issue of African Wildlife.

USHER, G., 1970. *A dictionary of botany.* Constable, London.

VAN DER SCHIJFF, H. P. and SCHOONRAAD, E., 1971 *The flora of Mariepskop complex. Bothalia* 10 part 3. Dept. of Agricultural Technical Services, Pretoria.

VAN DER SCHIJFF, H. P., 1969. *A checklist of the vascular plants of the Kruger National Park.* Publications of the University of Pretoria, New series 53. Van Schaik, Pretoria.

VAN DER WALT, J. J. A., 1973. *The South African species of Commiphora. Bothalia* 11 no. 1 and 2. Dept. of Agricultural Technical Services, Pretoria.

VAN DER WALT, J. J. A., 1977. *Pelargoniums of Southern Africa.* Purnell, Cape Town.

VAN WYK, P., 1972 and 1974. *Trees of the Kruger National Park* 1 and 2. Purnell, Cape Town.

VERDOORN, I. C., 1973. *The genus Crinum in South Africa. Bothalia* 11 no. 1 and 2. Dept. of Agricultural Technical Services, Pretoria.

VISSER, J., 1981. *South African parasitic flowering plants.* Juta, Cape Town.

VON BREITENBACH, F. and J., 1974. *Baobab flower. Trees in S.A.,* Journal of the Tree Society of Southern Africa 26 part 1, Johannesburg.

WATT, J. M. and BREYER-BRANDWIJK, M. G., 1962. *The medicinal and poisonous plants of Southern and Eastern Africa.* 2nd edition. E. & S. Livingstone, Edinburgh and London.

WIENS, D. and TÖLKEN, H. R., 1979. *Loranthaceae. Flora of Southern Africa* 10 part 1. Dept. of Agricultural Technical Services, Pretoria.

About the Botanical Society of South Africa

Founded in 1913 at the same time as Kirstenbosch Botanic Garden, the Botanical Society aims to interest the people of South Africa and other countries in the National Botanic Gardens. We also aim to educate members of the public in the cultivation, conservation and awareness of our unique indigenous flora.

Are you a member?

The Botanical Society of South Africa is one of the largest, most effective organisations working to safeguard our veld and flora. If you are not already a member we invite you to join. There is something for everyone in the Society's wide range of activities, from hikes and walks to illustrated lectures, tours and conservation activism. Members receive the colourful and informative "Veld & Flora" magazine, free seeds of your choice annually from the Kirstenbosch seedlist, 10% discount on books from our bookshop as well as free admission to all the national botanic gardens in South Africa.

By joining the Society you support those members who are willing to invest their time and expertise to protect our natural heritage for this and future generations. We need your membership and support. To join, please contact the Executive Secretary, Botanical Society of South Africa, Kirstenbosch, Claremont 7735 R.S.A. or telephone Cape Town (021) 771725.

Any donations or bequests made to the Botanical Society or its Flora Conservation Committee are free of donations and estate duty tax.